GREAT LIVES OBSERVED

Gerald Emanuel Stearn, *General Editor*

EACH VOLUME IN THE SERIES VIEWS THE CHARACTER AND ACHIEVE-
MENT OF A GREAT WORLD FIGURE IN THREE PERSPECTIVES—
THROUGH HIS OWN WORDS, THROUGH THE OPINIONS OF HIS CON-
TEMPORARIES, AND THROUGH RETROSPECTIVE JUDGMENTS—THUS
COMBINING THE INTIMACY OF AUTOBIOGRAPHY, THE IMMEDIACY
OF EYE-WITNESS OBSERVATION, AND THE OBJECTIVITY OF MODERN
SCHOLARSHIP.

MARTIN GILBERT, *the editor of this volume in the Great Lives
Observed series, is a Fellow of Merton College, Oxford, and
Senior Research Assistant to Randolph S. Churchill on the
Official Life of Sir Winston Churchill. He is the author of
numerous influential works, including* The European Powers
1900-1945, The Roots of Appeasement, Britain and Germany
Between the Wars, *and a* Recent History Atlas. *He edited* A
Century of Conflict: Essays for A. J. P. Taylor, *and is Recent
History Correspondent for the London* Sunday Times.

Forthcoming volumes in the Great Lives Observed series

Elizabeth I, *edited by Joseph Levine*

John Calhoun, *edited by Margaret L. Coit*

Hitler, *edited by George Stein*

Lincoln, *edited by James P. Shenton*

Lloyd George, *edited by Martin Gilbert*

Luther, *edited by Paul A. Lee*

Mao, *edited by Jerome Ch'en*

GREAT LIVES OBSERVED

CHURCHILL

Edited by MARTIN GILBERT

Mr. Churchill,
What brought you into politics?
Ambition
What keeps you there?
Anger

A SPECTRUM BOOK

PRENTICE-HALL, INC., ENGLEWOOD CLIFFS, N.J.

Preface

I would like to thank my wife Helen who scrutinized the text and made many valuable suggestions; David Hoffman, who gave me the benefit of an American view and was ever ready to advise; Ivor Samuels, whose help was, as always, a great encouragement; and Mrs. Devika Holloway who transformed rough drafts into neat typescript and enabled the book to be written with the minimum of chaos.

MARTIN GILBERT

Contents

Introduction   1

Chronology of the Life of Churchill   14

PART ONE

CHURCHILL LOOKS AT THE WORLD

1

War   16

The Ugliness of War, *17* The Dull, Dark Clouds of
Militarism, *20* England on the Eve of War, *24* Will
Our Children Bleed and Gasp Again? *25* "The Clear
Path of Duty," *26* "In War, Resolution . . . In Peace,
Goodwill," *28*

2

Government and Reform   30

The New Role of the State, *30* "The Unnatural Gap
Between Rich and Poor," *34* Attacking the House of
Lords, *35* Tonypandy, *37* The Foundations of De-
mocracy, *38*

3

Empire   39

Constructive Imperialism, *40* British Rights in India, *42*
"The Clattering Down of the British Empire," *44*

4

World Affairs   **46**

No Cause for War, *46* "Repair the Waste. Rebuild the Ruins," *48* Death Stands at Attention, *50* Arms for Peace, *54* "An Iron Curtain Has Descended," *55*

5

Defiance   **59**

"We Shall Never Surrender," *59* The Fall of France, *60* Awaiting the German Invasion, *61* "Re-Arm Your Spirits," *63* "All Will Come Right," *65* A Call to America: "Time Is Short," *67* Alliance with Russia: "This Is No Class War," *70* The Grand Alliance: "The Sleep of the Saved," *73*

PART TWO
THE WORLD LOOKS AT CHURCHILL

G. W. Steevens: Born to Lead, *75* Consuelo Vanderbilt: "The Democratic Spirit," *79* St. John Brodrick: Rebuke for the Renegade, *79* Wilfrid Scawen Blunt: "A Strange Replica of His Father," *80* A. J. Balfour: Advice to a Young Critic, *81* MacCallum Scott: The Champion of Liberalism, *81* Theodore Roosevelt: A Warm Dislike, *83* A. G. Gardiner: "In the Thick of the Fight," *84* Lord Riddell: The Other Side of Churchill, *87* The New York *World*: In Defense of Churchill, *87* H. H. Asquith: "He Will Never Get to the Top," *88* Lord Hankey: Confidence and Energy in War, *89* David Lloyd George: Churchill in Eclipse, *90* Andrew Dewar Gibb: Churchill at the Front, *91* A. G. Gardiner: "Keep Your Eye on Churchill," *93* David Lloyd George: Conservatives Could Not Forgive, *99* Blackwood's Magazine: The Dog Has His Day, *103* Lord Beaverbrook: "A Foot in Both Camps," *105* H. G. Wells: "I Want to See Him Out," *106* Fenner Brockway: "A Public Danger and a Menace to Peace," *107* Victor Germains: A Brilliant

Failure, *108* Lord Birkenhead: "The Force of Sheer Genius," *111* Lord D'Abernon: "A Mind of Great Fertility," *116* Emanuel Shinwell: Labour Looks at Churchhill, *120* Harold Nicolson: "The Most Interesting Man in England," *124* Sir Arthur Salter: The Wilderness Years, *125* Vincent Sheean: A Mind Tempered for Crisis, *126* Stanley Baldwin: Eloquence Without Wisdom, *129* Adolf Hitler: "Churchill, Feel Yourself Honored," *130* Louis Fischer: "The Total Impression Is Power," *131* Viscount Montgomery: "He Must Dominate," *133* Aneurin Bevan: Keeping Churchill in Check, *134* Alan Herbert: "Sensitive as well as Tough," *135* H. G. Wells: Time to Retire, *136* Leslie Hore-Belisha: "He Meant Business," *137*

PART THREE
CHURCHILL IN RETROSPECT

Lady Violet Bonham-Carter:
"Defiant Snooks at All Authority"   144

Isaiah Berlin: Churchill and Roosevelt   150

Leopold Amery: Churchill and Lloyd George   154

Sir Arthur Bryant: Churchill and
His Chief of Staff   157

John F. Kennedy: "He Has Always
Championed Liberty"   162

Harold Wilson: "The Qualities Born in Him"   164

The New Statesman: "Incapable
of Using Power Evilly"   167

Afterword   170

Bibliographical Note   173

Index   177

GREAT LIVES OBSERVED

CHURCHILL

Introduction

Churchill's life story poses a difficult problem: that of the interpretation of a statesman's actions through sixty years of political ferment. Was he consistent, was he sincere, was he profound, had he ability, had he wisdom, did he understand the intricate problems of the world order he sought to preserve, did he understand the aspirations and needs of the individuals he professed to champion, was he prepared to make sacrifices in order to resist the dangers which he thought were about to challenge and even engulf the systems of government in which he believed? How do we interpret his widely differing spheres of action; how do we relate his warnings and prophesies to the needs and realities of society; how do we measure the man and assess his contributions to his country and the world? In this volume I seek the answers in an analysis of his career, in a study of his own speeches and writings, in contemporary judgments, and in retrospective comments.

My view is that Churchill was a statesman of vision and ability, a genius who for sixty years put his many gifts at the disposal of his fellow countrymen and of mankind. It is for the reader to judge, with the help of the documents selected, whether this is a fair assessment. I have chosen extracts which I believe are representative of the wide range of his own life and of the views of contemporaries.

Winston Churchill was born at Blenheim Palace, Oxfordshire, in England in 1874. He died, aged 90, in 1965, in his London home. His maternal grandfather was an American millionaire, Leonard Jerome, and through him, American Indian blood as well as that of a revolutionary heritage ran in his veins. His paternal grandfather was an English Duke, direct descendent of John Churchill, Duke of Marlborough, who had won a series of decisive military victories against King Louis XIV of France at the beginning of the eighteenth century, and of whom it was said that he besieged no fortress that he did not capture and began no battle that he did not win.

These were two powerful ancestries. Singly, they might have produced a man of stature, for his grandfather Jerome was a business-

1

man of acumen and eccentricity, with wide interests in commerce, journalism, and sport, while his father Lord Randolph Churchill was a politician of remarkable powers, an outspoken and fearless critic of mediocrity and hypocrisy, a political rebel with a sharp temper and a biting tongue. Once combined, these bloodstreams produced a potent synthesis, a dynamo equipped with limitless energy, sweeping imagination, tough perseverance, and uncanny foresight. From his father he acquired the traditions of the English aristocracy: self-confidence, ambition, and a desire to get to the root of the matter. From his mother, Jennie Jerome, came that pioneering spirit, that total lack of pretence, that hatred of snobbery, and that belief in the powers of one's own star and in the importance of one's personal abilities which had driven forward to a series of new frontiers the men and women who had built the United States.

Those who met Winston Churchill during his long lifetime were immediately struck by his unusual character. His personality made an impact even before his ideas had fully developed, and certainly before he had achieved political stature. Not only the wars he went to in India and Africa as a young man, but the books which he at once wrote about them, and the controversies over them into which he immediately plunged without pausing for fear of rebuke, drew him swiftly to the nation's attention. His writings were prolific and outspoken. Before he was twenty-five he had attacked with equal vigor the cruelty of war, the stupidity of generals, the inadequacy of government, and the pettiness of prudery.

Once in Parliament, though one of the most junior members, he became immediately a center of stern controversy. Some resented his frankness. Others criticized his self-confidence. Ally and critic, journalist and newspaper reader, all spoke of him as "Winston." He became a household word before he was thirty. And for the following sixty years, whatever he said or did—and he was seldom either silent or inactive—became the focal point of wide and often bitter comment. Many feared his strong opinions and the clarity with which he expressed them. Many doubted that he was as wise or as mature as he sounded. Many were hurt by his censures, for his criticisms were acute. The antagonisms, rancor, and sullen hostility of those whose ideas or activities he had attacked were long-lived. A vast ground swell of resentment hindered and at times disrupted the smooth flow of his career. His life was a stormy one, made so by his own energies. He was never still. He was never complacent. He was seldom content with what he saw around him. Throughout his life he made enemies. Few public men in any nation can have incurred so full a measure of hostility. Yet he persevered. He was seldom downhearted or depressed. He never wavered, even when his warnings, as of Adolf Hitler's aggressive intentions in the 1930s, were disbelieved or ignored by the majority of Englishmen. Nor did he lose, despite this ever present lack of trust in him, a faith in his star. This faith enabled him to survive political setbacks and cruel accusations which would have driven most men out of public life entirely. He preserved also, amid all the storms and shipwrecks of his life, a puckish smile, a disarming sense of humor, and that striking magnanimity which many contemporaries considered his greatest attribute. He forgave his enemies and harbored no malice toward past opponents. Rancor and hatred were emotions that seldom touched him. He was incapable of deceit and often failed to recognize it in others, which made him somewhat gullible. Nothing mattered for him but to pursue his goals. He never allowed personal animosities on his part to stand in his way. Sometimes he succeeded in dispelling the hostility which critics felt toward him. But despite his magnanimity and charm, the malice and mistrust of others was a burden which he bore throughout his life.

The Britain into whose political life Churchill plunged in 1900 was a troubled land. The gulf between rich and poor, which had so alarmed Disraeli sixty years earlier, remained the greatest indictment of industrialization and free enterprise. "Society" was rich, gay, and indolent; the laboring classes were exploited and depressed. The ruling Conservative Party conducted government business with lethargic complacency. The Labour Party was in its infancy, and drew what influence it had entirely from the working class. Only the Liberal Party seemed capable of vigorous, root-and-branch reform. But it too lacked dynamic personalities capable of challenging convention, and its one striking figure, David Lloyd George, who had made his mark in a series of attacks on the "wicked imperialism" of the Boer War, was himself young.

When Churchill became a Member of Parliament he was a Conservative. But he soon found the Party too slow a vehicle for his purpose. Within five years he had changed over to the Liberal Party, and was attacking Conservatives with some of the most outspoken invective in the history of Parliament. These attacks brought upon him the life-long enmity of many Conservatives; they also showed the nation that he was not a man to mince his words or hide his feelings. The Conservative Ministers, he taunted, "are ready to make great sacrifices for their opinions, but they have no opinions. They are ready to die for the truth, if only they knew what the truth was." And again: "To keep office for a few more months there is no principle which the Government are not prepared to betray, and no quantity of dust and filth they are not prepared to eat." For twenty years Churchill, often in close partnership with Lloyd George, dominated the Liberal Party, driving it into bold social reform which changed the character of Britain, and pushing it into a state of naval preparedness which served Britain well when Germany invaded France and Belgium, and sought a hegemony in Europe in 1914.

Churchill's record as a social reformer was remarkable, an achievement which future historians may well rank with his war leadership. In 1940, by his speeches and example, he roused the British nation, preserved its unity, and personified its defiance. Thirty years earlier he had striven to bring about a revolution—to eliminate social injustice and to provide State securities against illness, widowhood, and unemployment. He had succeeded in introducing into Government legislation a new mood of humanity toward the daily life of workingmen, and toward the problems of those who, through accident or crime, had fallen foul of society. As President of the Board of Trade he showed, in the words of one historian, "conspicuous gifts as a planner, organizer, and administrator . . . in particular his faculty of drafting large-scale projects while at the same time supervising their execution down to minute detail." He applied his mind to the black spots of British society with almost feverish dedication, and indeed relish. He never made heavy weather of his difficult tasks, in peace or in war. Hard work was his joy; problems were his delight. The greater the problem to be tackled, the greater his relish at the task before him.

Merely to enumerate some of his achievements at this time, over a period of only four years, is to realize the practicality and range of his genius. As his first major social legislation he introduced a bill to Parliament which gave coal miners a maximum working day of eight hours. This measure was long overdue and had been debated for twenty years. Churchill made it the law of the land. He had been amazed, he told the House of Commons while explaining the reform, not by the demands of the miners, "but by the gentleman in the silk hat and white waistcoat who has the composure and the complacency to deny that demand and dispute it with him." Churchill then piloted the Trade Boards Bill through Parliament. By this legislation, minimum wages were fixed by law in trades where previously profits had been inflated by cheap sweated labor, and in particular by the misuse of Jewish immigrant labor. As a result of Churchill's efforts, two hundred thousand workers on the margin of poverty were given immediate State protection and wage improvement. He then turned to the problem of unemployment: "We simply have to solve the problem of the man searching desperately for work and unable to find it—because he does not know when and where work can be found, and has no means of knowing." Churchill provided the means, Labour Exchanges, and he made them a direct State responsibility. Within two years their network spread over the country, a security for workers and an advantage to employers which has continued to this day. While at the Board of Trade, he proposed to the Government that they introduce a comprehensive scheme of Unemployment Insurance. "If I had my way," he told an audience at Manchester, "I would write the word 'Insure' over the door of every cottage, and upon the blotting-book of every public man." The National Insurance Act, a masterpiece of social legislation, was then evolved partly by Churchill, partly by Lloyd George. Although it has been written of as Lloyd George's greatest achievement, it is equally a monument to Churchill—to his foresight and to his application to detail.

When he became Home Secretary in 1910 Churchill's activities flourished in another sphere—the administration of justice. In 1909 over 95,000 people were sent to prison for failing to pay fines. Churchill considered this an abuse of the powers of imprisonment, and despite the reluctance of his officials, made it possible for those who were fined to have "time to pay." Henceforth this liberal decision was accepted as a principle of national policy. By 1919 there were only 5,000 people imprisoned as fine-defaulters. He also altered the law in relation to young people so that many fewer between the ages of sixteen and twenty-one were sent to prison, and he laid down the ruling that no young person was to receive "a sentence that is merely punitive," but that any imprisonment should aim to be "positively of a curative and educative character." He improved the conditions of prison life, providing more exercise and the possibility of food from outside. He introduced lectures and concerts. And he reduced the maximum period of solitary confinement to one month. "The changes," wrote *The Times* in July 1910, "are one and all inspired by imagination, without which reform is deadly, and by common sense, without which it is dangerous." Thus Churchill ameliorated the lives of his fellow countrymen, and in particular those who suffered hardship or injustice. His was the humane and tolerant eye, able to see in an instant what could be done, willing to devote his own energies to doing it, wise enough to prepare it comprehensively and clearly, free from humbug and free from cant, and forceful enough to make it the law of the land.

Superficially it would seem that Churchill's career was an entirely successful one. He was an active legislator during a vigorous period of social reform; he directed first the Navy and then the production of Munitions during World War I; he was subsequently, in peacetime, in charge first of the Army and the Air Force, then of Britain's Colonies, and finally of the Treasury. Then, after a ten-year gap, he returned to direct the Navy at the outbreak of World War II, and when the course of the war worsened he became Prime Minister, held the post with honor for five years, and was later Prime Minister for a second time. Surely a success story with no parallel in English history? High office over a period of nearly fifty years; a variety of fascinating experiences; the fulfillment of ambition's boldest dream: what story could be less gloomy, what life more glamorous? Yet the responsible positions which Churchill held, and the heights to which he rose, were reached by no easy or obvious road. His whole political career was an uphill struggle. Nor was it at all certain at any given moment of that struggle that he would prevail. Throughout the forty years between his entering Parliament and his becoming Prime Minister he suffered a series of major setbacks. His footsteps were dogged by frequent and strident accusations of past mistakes. His explanations were mostly disbelieved, the evidence which he produced was ignored. For those critics, and there were always many of them, who wished to think that whatever Churchill touched he would destroy, historical accuracy was of no

importance. Contemporaries and historians alike have been curiously reluctant to examine dispassionately the facts of his life's work,
and to cast a neutral eye upon the evidence of the crisis moments in
his career.

One of the blackest marks against Churchill has been "Tonypandy," a name always produced to prove his love of bloodshed.
In 1910 serious rioting broke out among strikers in the Welsh min-
ing town of Tonypandy. The local authorities, unable to quell the
riot with the police at their disposal, asked for troops. The soldiers
were on their way to Wales by train when Churchill was informed
of the affair. As Home Secretary he was ultimately responsible for
maintaining law and order, and for the use of soldiers in time of
national emergency. His first act was to halt the troop trains and
to insist that the soldiers detrain. Then he ordered a detachment of
London policemen to Wales to help quell the riot. They were unarmed, and the only "weapons" they were authorized to use were
their rolled-up raincoats. The riots were halted. Not a single life
was lost. Yet socialist newspapers portrayed Churchill as the man
most eager to force a clash between strikers and soldiers. To this day
the legend persists, particularly in Labour circles, that Churchill's
action led to actual bloodshed. Strange as it may now seem, while
socialists raised the cry of "warmonger," Conservatives tried to
embarrass Churchill politically by accusing him of the reverse, for he
was at once attacked in *The Times* for undue leniency. In Parliament he defended his moderation on the grounds that if troops
ever fired upon workers it would be "a catastrophe in our national
life." Churchill's aim was never to suppress strikes as such, but to
halt destructive riots in which strikers were prominent. At the time
his action was frowned upon by Conservatives because it was too
mild. When, eight months later, a strike on the railways led to
further serious riots at Liverpool, and rioters prevented vital sup-
plies of food from reaching hospitals, the local police again demanded troops to help them in their duty and to protect them
from mob violence. After some hesitation Churchill agreed to send
troops, but they were ordered to fire over the heads of the crowd,
which they did. The strike ended without a single fatality in Liverpool. The only deaths came in South Wales after the strike had
been settled: a mob in Llanelly had halted and looted a train,
having beaten the engineer unconscious. Troops were called in to

prevent further bloodshed and two rioters were killed while refusing to disperse.

Churchill acted throughout these grave civil disturbances with moderation and care. His principal aim throughout was to restore order without undue use of force, and to ensure the minimum loss of life. This he achieved. Yet it has ever since been held, not only that he took the initiative in setting troops against workers, but also that he relished the idea of a violent clash between the two. Both views are false. Yet A. J. P. Taylor, the author of the 1914-1945 volume of the *Oxford History of England,* writes of Churchill at this time as "the most aggressive minister against the workers," and Lord Dalton, a former Labour Cabinet minister and wartime colleague of Churchill's, in an obituary notice, criticized him for his action "at Tonypandy in 1910 when he used troops against miners on strike." Both these men should have known better; neither took the trouble to check the facts; both were victims of an anti-Churchill legend which was built up over the years. The cry "Remember Tonypandy" was always hurled at him on public platforms. The belief that he enjoyed shooting workers survived even after World War II, when one might have expected a certain reluctance to accept old legends. It flourishes today, when there is absolutely no excuse for it to do so.

Other names flung at Churchill in anger at public meetings, and echoed with disapproval in many history books, were "Antwerp" and "Gallipoli." Again, the verdict of accurate history will probably be to his advantage. At Antwerp he tried, with full Cabinet approval, to persuade the Belgian Government to resist the attacking Germans for a few more days, while, further back, the forces of the Allies regrouped in order to meet more effectively the German onslaught. Churchill's mission was a success: the city held out for the extra days, and the German advance was slowed down. It was a small incident of the war, and one in which Churchill had acted energetically and sensibly, encouraged by his colleagues and welcomed by the Belgians. Yet even while he was still on his difficult mission the Conservative press were attacking what they claimed were his irresponsibility, his adventures, his childish capers, and his desire for self-advertisement. The accusations stuck, and grew over the years. A responsible and in many ways decisive act by a public servant in the national interest became construed as a piece of frivolous folly. As A. J. P. Taylor points out, "his name was tarnished by Antwerp"; yet Taylor himself adds to the tarnish by his description of the incident as one of irresponsible action with no serious effect. He considers that the German delay at Antwerp probably prevented them from winning the race to the sea; then he ascribes that delay as "due rather to the Belgian defense than to Churchill." Yet it is clear from the records that it was Churchill's arguments which finally persuaded the Belgians to persevere in the city's defense. The problem of historical interpretation is, of course, a difficult one. Historians are always likely to disagree over the meaning of particular facts. But Churchill has had more than his share of misinterpretation. At every crisis moment of his career, many contemporaries and historians tended to draw an anti-Churchill lesson, and seldom give Churchill the benefit either of the doubt or of the evidence.

"Gallipoli" was Churchill's plan to end World War I as quickly as possible. It depended upon a naval victory at the Dardanelles, the capture of the Turkish town of Gallipoli, and the appearance of the British Fleet off Constantinople. If Turkey were defeated so early in the war, the neutral Balkan states might have thrown in their lot with the Allies and been a grave threat to Austria, while Russia, relieved of Turkish military pressure in the Caucasus, could have thrown her full weight against Germany. It was a bold scheme, and it was approved by the British Cabinet. It failed because of bad planning at a local level, and because of the obstinate refusal of Lord Kitchener, the War Secretary, to cooperate fully. Those who fought there, like the future Labour Prime Minister Clement Attlee, felt that Churchill's strategic conception was a sound one. Certainly its aim was to hasten the end of the war, thus saving millions of lives. But Churchill was henceforward known as the man who had risked Allied lives in a reckless adventure, and who had been motivated more by vainglory than by a realistic appraisal of the potential fields for decisive action.

Faced with so many unjust criticisms, and so little interest on the part of the anti-Churchill army in the historical details of events, it is always difficult to separate Churchill's achievements from his failures. His failures were many. Yet they should not be used to pour doubt on his achievements. Good judgment and error do not inhabit different planets. Churchill could be stubborn, strident, aggressive, and overassertive. He could exaggerate and abuse. He could pretend that a complex problem was a simple one, and thereby misunderstand it. Yet he never acted without the conviction that he was right, nor did he base his view of what was right on any tyrannical or aristocratic principle. He strongly disapproved of the exploitation of one class by another: he believed that everyone in a society had a right to rise by his own exertions. Indeed, it was this pugnacious concern for equality that led him into his most serious errors of judgment. In 1919 his dislike of the excesses of Bolshevik rule in Russia made him a foremost advocate of military intervention against Lenin. He encouraged the anti-Bolshevik Russian leaders to fight for Lenin's total overturn. He gave British military aid to the White Russian forces. He made fierce public speeches against the "baboonery of Bolshevism" and wrote with passion against communist doctrine. Few Englishmen consider this episode a creditable one in Churchill's career. It cast upon him derision and distrust in equal measure. Yet, in fairness to him it has to be admitted that in 1918 Bolshevism *was* a creed of violence and world revolution, and nothing that was known at that time in the west about conditions inside Russia or about Lenin's policies gave much cause for approval. Europe was alarmed at what evils communism might perpetrate, not only inside Russia but also westward into the war-weary nations seething with social unrest. Churchill's policy was supported by the Government: as Secretary of State for War he had to organize and explain the intervention. But he was not its sole advocate. It is also to his credit that as soon as some of the anti-Bolshevik armies revealed their fierce anti-Semitism, and began to persecute and murder the Jews of southern Russia, Churchill, almost alone of those in high office at the time, protested vigorously and withdrew his support.

What Churchill did wrong in 1919 was to identify himself so fiercely and uncompromisingly with what was, after all, Government policy. Thus in the public mind he became the sole anti-Bolshevik in the Cabinet. As he saw Lenin consolidate his power, Churchill's language became more extreme, more alarmist. This too gave the impression that he was unduly obsessed with Bolshevism. Yet who is to deny that at that time, with Europe half-starving, the defeated nations sullen, the victors at loggerheads over how to make peace, a series of Bolshevik revolutions might not have destroyed Europe as we know it, just as the war itself had destroyed four empires and brought to an end a way of life which may seem old-fashioned now, but which was at the time acceptable to many. Communist revolutions had succeeded in Hungary and Bavaria, and had appeared near success in Berlin and Vienna. Was Churchill so foolish as to feel that only by attacking what then seemed the new peril could it be kept from sweeping away the parliamentary democracies of Western Europe. As the historian A. L. Rowse has written:

> *It may not have been practical politics, but are many practical politicians capable to taking such long-term views, seeing events in historical perspective?* Looking at the history of the world since, at the sufferings men have endured from Lenin's seizure of power, the millions of lives sacrificed by it, *can one say that he was wrong? He was defeated, as often in his career—but that is quite a different matter.* He really detested tyranny of any kind, he loved freedom and free men. Perhaps that is why free men everywhere—not in Britain alone—rallied to him in the end.

With the problem of India the historian is confronted with the same dilemma. Churchill opposed Indian Independence in the 1930s because he feared that India was too divided by religious hatred to survive as a united nation if it became independent. Had he cared more for his reputation he would have kept silent over India. But, believing as he did that Britain's mission there was not at an end, that there were still benefits which Britain could confer, he again strove, openly and without disguising his strong feelings, to urge an unpopular course. Now it is unfashionable to praise imperial rule. Between the wars, however, there were still many for whom Empire was not an embarrassment or a crime, but a challenge and an opportunity. Churchill was one of these. Under British rule, as he pointed out, "War has been banished from India; her frontiers have been defended from the north; famine has been gripped and controlled. Justice has been given—equal between race and race, impartial between man and man." This was a noble vision. Churchill would certainly have liked to see it accepted as a true picture of British rule in India. He had not created the weaknesses and blemishes of imperialism. Nor should we be too quick to condemn him for seeking to preserve an institution which he hoped would benefit all religious groups and would prevent the persecution of minorities.

Churchill's third serious breach with public sentiment was during the British General Strike of 1926. He abhorred the disruption of

the smooth working of society and clearly considered the strikers to
be acting against the national interest. He took charge of a newspaper which denounced them as the "enemy" and urged the nation
not to tolerate irresponsible strike action. But Churchill's role has
been greatly exaggerated. He was Chancellor of the Exchequer, at
the time, and had no control over the use of armored cars, which
was decided upon at the Home Office and by the Prime Minister.
Nor did he devise the final strikebreaking policy, which was entirely
evolved by Baldwin and his civil servant advisers. Churchill was
thought to be the leading "militant," but when the strike was
over it was he who took the lead in trying to meet the griev-
ances of the miners, which had been the initial cause of the strike.
While he was Chancellor of the Exchequer Churchill introduced
further measures of social reform which benefited the less well-
to-do: a lower income-tax demand for small incomes, a Government
pension scheme for widows, and higher death duties for the rich.

Between 1930 and 1939 Churchill was severely criticized because
he spoke frequently and clearly in favor of British rearmament. He
feared that if Britain were to remain weak, the dictator nations
would seek to gain territory by conquest. He opposed the conquest
of one nation by another and was revolted by Nazi persecutions.
He urged the democracies to combine for their own defense. But he
was speaking in a wilderness, and his warnings fell on stony ground.
Some historians have echoed contemporaries in saying that he was
being too much of an alarmist. But the dangers were great, and all
his life he was incapable of prevarication.

It would be wrong to judge a historical figure solely by the standards of the present day. Every generation has its own morality. The
historian is not primarily a judge who drags people from out of
their environment and places them before a contemporary tribunal.
His first aim is to see whether the people he studies acted for the
good of their own society, as they envisaged that good. His second
aim is to ask whether the ideas which he is examining are valid in
terms of present values. Although Churchill lived until 1965, his
education and youthful environment were very different from our
own. The things which he and his contemporaries took for granted
at the turn of the century are no longer the basic beliefs of society
—a faith in the uninterrupted evolution of social improvement, an
acceptance of kings and emperors as the natural rulers of much of

mankind, a faith in the power of imperialism to improve the lot of primitive or backward people, and a conviction that war between civilized, industrialized states would never come to pass. All these precepts were part of the air men breathed; now they are anachronisms.

Churchill cannot be condemned for breathing the air around him. Yet he was sufficiently different to lack certain conventional traits. He had many Jewish friends at a time when Jews were barely accepted among the upper classes, and he was one of the earliest supporters of a Jewish national home in Palestine. He did not seek to halt Germany's growing power before 1914; rather, he welcomed it as an accession to the strength and stability of the civilized world. He did not rest content, as did many of his contemporaries, with the harsh workings of industrial society; instead he believed that the State should intervene decisively whenever private enterprise proved unable to eradicate social evils. He believed in the responsibility of the State toward all its subjects, despite the pressure in the opposite direction which his social standing and environment might well have dictated. He served his country to the best of his ability in peace and war through sixty years. He warned of danger when he believed danger to be near and inspired courage when courage was needed. He always believed in democratic institutions and fought fearlessly to preserve them. He hated intolerance and injustice. He survived the accumulated malice of four decades to win the affection not only of Englishmen but of free men everywhere. This was no passing show, no momentary skill. He dominated the world he lived in, not by tyranny but by his abilities and his opinions. He fulfilled Demosthenes' dictum:

> The statesman declares his mind before the event and submits himself to be tested by those who have believed in him. The politician is silent when he ought to have spoken.

In this volume I seek to show what he did and why he did it. I try also to see him as his contemporaries saw him, now in a good light, now in a bad one. It is for the reader to judge, with the aid of the material presented here, whether he would place Churchill in the first rank of statesmen.

Chronology of the
Life of Churchill

1874	(November 30) Born at Blenheim Palace, Oxfordshire, son of Lord Randolph Churchill and Jennie Jerome.
1888-93	Studies at Harrow School. Excels at swimming, fencing, history, and essay writing—but not at Latin.
1893-94	Cavalry cadet at Sandhurst Royal Military College.
1895	Father dies. Visits Cuba to study fighting between Spain and rebels. Writes first newspaper article on the fighting.
1896-97	On active service in India with Malakand Field Force. Educates himself by reading history, philosophy and politics. Writes book on the Malakand campaign.
1898	Serves in cavalry during reconquest of Sudan. Fights in battle of Omdurman. Writes his second book, *The River War*.
1899	Unsuccessful Conservative candidate at election.
1899-1900	Newspaper correspondent at Boer War in South Africa. Taken prisoner and escapes. Returns to England a hero. Publishes two books on the war and a novel, *Savrola*. Elected Conservative Member of Parliament for Oldham. Lectures in the United States.
1903	Publishes an attack on the Conservative army scheme.
1904	Becomes a Liberal and attacks Conservatives bitterly.
1906	Publishes biography of his father. Receives first Government office, Under-Secretary of State for the Colonies.
1907	Becomes Privy Councillor: styled the Right Honourable.
1908	Enters Cabinet as President of the Board of Trade. Marries Clementine Hozier.
1910	Home Secretary.
1911-15	First Lord of the Admiralty.
1915	Chancellor of the Duchy of Lancaster.
1915-16	Serves with Army on the western front.
1917	Made Minister of Munitions by Lloyd George.
1919	Secretary of State for War and Air. Supervises demobilization.
1921	Colonial Secretary. Helps negotiate Irish Treaty.
1922	Defeated in General Election; out of Parliament.
1923	Publishes first of five-volume history of the war.

1924	Reelected to Parliament. Changes back to Conservatives after twenty years as a Liberal.
1924-29	Chancellor of the Exchequer. Introduces five national Budgets.
1926	Organizes *British Gazette* newspaper during General Strike.
1929	Out of office; visits Canada and the United States.
1930	Breach with Conservative Party over India policy: finds himself in political wilderness. Publishes his memoirs, *A Roving Commission.*
1931	Lecture tour in United States. Knocked down by taxi in New York and badly hurt.
1932	Publishes volume of essays, *Amid These Storms.*
1933	Publishes first of four-volume life of his ancestor, Duke of Marlborough.
1936-39	Warns against danger of disarmament. Urges defensive alliance of democracies. Speaks against Munich agreement. Publishes two more volumes of speeches and articles.
1939	On outbreak of war, becomes First Lord of the Admiralty.
1940	(May 10) Prime Minister.
1941	Atlantic meeting with President Roosevelt.
1942	Visits Washington, Cairo, and Moscow for war conferences.
1943	Visits Washington and addresses Congress.
1944	Visits French and Italian fronts.
1945	(February) At Yalta with Stalin and Roosevelt. (July) Defeated at General Election. Leader of Opposition in Parliament.
1946	Fulton speech warns of East-West rift.
1948	First volume of six-volume history of World War II published.
1951-55	Prime Minister for second time.
1953	Made Knight of the Garter; henceforth styled Sir Winston. Awarded Nobel Prize for literature and oratory.
1956	In retirement at age of 82, publishes first of four-volume *History of the English-Speaking Peoples.*
1963	Made Honorary Citizen of the United States.
1965	(January 24) Dies in London. Buried in Bladon Churchyard, near Blenheim Palace.

PART ONE

CHURCHILL LOOKS AT THE WORLD

1

War

Revenge is, of all satisfactions, the most costly and long drawn-out; retributive persecution is, of all policies, the most pernicious.

—CHURCHILL

Let us learn our lessons. Never, never, never believe any war will be smooth and easy, or that anyone who embarks on that strange voyage can measure the tides and hurricanes he will encounter. The Statesman who yields to war fever must realize that once the signal is given, he is no longer the master of policy but the slave of unforeseeable and uncontrollable events.

—CHURCHILL

When people think of Churchill they think of war. No man in British, or even American history, has been regarded as so exact an embodiment of the spirit of combat. He has been portrayed often as the warmaker of the Western world. This view is a mistaken one. Certainly it was Churchill's lifelong belief that, if one's country was at war, all the nation's energy should be concentrated upon a single aim: "Victory—victory at all costs, victory in spite of all terror, victory however long and hard the road may be." But the object of victory was survival, not destruction. Churchill had no sympathy for warmaking as such. He had no relish for senseless or indiscriminate slaughter. Indeed, for him, war was the supreme human catastrophe. He saw clearly, from an early age, that war was a terrible curse, which inevitably brought personal hardship and physical destruction in its wake. Nor did he gloat over victory when it came. He gained no pleasure from seeing his enemies destroyed and their cities reduced to rubble. As he said in March 1945, on the eve of the end of the war in Europe:

16

"Victory lies before us, certain and perhaps near. But years of cruel torment and destruction have wasted the earth, and victory with all its brilliant trappings appears to our strained and experienced eyes as a deliverance rather than a triumph."

THE UGLINESS OF WAR [1]

Churchill's personal experience of war began in Cuba in 1897, where he watched at close quarters the Spanish government suppressing an anti-imperialist revolt. Within two years he had fought in the British Army in India and Africa. It was from this experience that he drew the lessons which were to guide him all his life. His description of the aftermath of the Battle of Omdurman, in the Sudan, gives a stark and sombre picture of the horror of war. Churchill and a fellow junior officer are crossing the battlefield three days after the battle.

We galloped on. A strong, hot wind blew from the west across the great plain and hurried foul and tainted to the river. Keeping to windward of the thickest clusters, we picked our way, and the story of the fight unfolded itself. Here was where the artillery had opened on the swarming masses. Men had fallen in little groups of five or six to each shell. Nearer to the zeriba—about 1,000 yards from it—the musketry had begun to tell, and the dead lay evenly scattered about—one every ten yards. Two hundred yards further the full force of the fire—artillery, Maxims and rifles—had burst on them. In places desperate rushes to get on at all costs had been made by devoted, fearless men. In such places the bodies lay so thickly as to hide the ground. Occasionally there were double layers of this hideous covering. Once I saw them lying three deep. In a space not exceeding a hundred yards square more than 400 corpses lay festering.

It is difficult to imagine the postures into which man, once created in the image of his Maker, had been twisted. It is not wise to try,

[1] From Winston S. Churchill, *The River War* (London and New York, 1900), II, 220-26. Reprinted by permission of Odhams Press Limited, proprietors of the copyright. In every case of Churchill's own writings the first English edition has been cited and referred to. A full list of his books published in the United States will be found in the bibliography.

for he who succeeds will ask himself with me: 'Can I ever forget?'

I have tried to gild war, and to solace myself for the loss of dear and gallant friends, with the thought that a soldier's death for a cause that he believes in will count for much, whatever may be beyond this world. When the soldier of a civilised Power is killed in action, his limbs are composed and his body is borne by friendly arms reverently to the grave. The wail of the fifes, the roll of the drums, the triumphant words of the Funeral Service, all divest the act of its squalor; and the spectator sympathises with, perhaps almost envies, the comrade who has found this honourable exit. But there was nothing *dulce et decorum* about the Dervish dead; nothing of the dignity of unconquerable manhood; all was filthy corruption. Yet these were as brave men as ever walked the earth. The conviction was borne in on me that their claim beyond the grave in respect of a valiant death was not less good than that which any of our countrymen could make. The thought may not be original; it may happily be untrue; it seemed certainly most unwelcome.

The incidents of the battle might be traced by the lines and patches of the slain. Here was where MacDonald's brigade, the three artillery batteries, and eight Maxim guns had repulsed the Khalifa's attack. A great heap of corpses lay round the spot where the Black Flag had been captured. There was where the brigade had faced about to meet Ali-Wad-Helu and Osman Sheikh-ed-Din. There, again, was where the Baggara cavalry had made their last splendid charge to certain death. The white-clad bodies of the men were intermingled with the brown and bay horses, so that this part of the field looked less white-speckled than the rest. They had ridden straight at the solid line of bayonets and in the teeth of the storm of projectiles. Every man had galloped at full speed, and when he fell he shot many lengths in front of his horse, rolling over and over—destroyed, not conquered, by machinery.

At such sights the triumph of victory faded on the mind, and a mournful feeling of disgust grew stronger. All this was bad to see, but worse remained; after the dead, the wounded. The officer or soldier who escapes from the field with a wound has a claim on his country. To the private it may mean a pension; to the officer a gratuity, perhaps a 'mention in despatches,' certainly advancement in his profession. The scar may even, when the sting has departed, be a source of pride—an excuse to re-tell the story. To soothe the pain there are anaesthetics; to heal the injury the resources of science are at hand. It was otherwise with the Dervish wounded.

There may have been wounded Dervishes among the heaps of slain. The atmosphere forbade approach. There certainly were many scattered about the plain. We approached these cautiously and, pistol in hand, examined their condition. Lord Tullibardine had a large water-bottle. He dismounted, and gave a few drops to each till it was all gone. You must remember that this was three days after the fight, and that the sun had beaten down mercilessly all the time. Some of the wounded were very thirsty. It would have been a grateful sight to see a large bucket of clear, cool water placed before each shaking, feverish figure. That, or a nameless man with a revolver and a big bag of cartridges, would have seemed merciful. The scenes were pathetic. Where there was a shady bush four men had crawled to die. Someone had spread a rag on the thorns to increase the shade. Three of the unfortunate creatures had attained their object; the fourth survived. He was shot through both legs. The bullet—a Martini-Henry bullet—had lodged in the right knee-cap. The whole limb was stiffened. We gave him a drink. You would not think such joy could come from a small cup of water. Tullibardine examined his injury. Presently he pulled out his knife, and after much probing and cutting extracted the bullet—with the button-hook. I have seen, and shall see perchance again, a man with a famous name worse employed.

Would the reader be further sickened with the horrors of the field? There was a man that had crawled a mile in three days, but was yet two miles from the river. He had one foot; the other remained behind. I wonder if he ever reached the water he had struggled so hard to attain! There was a man with both legs shattered; he had dragged himself along in a sitting posture, making perhaps four hundred yards a day. The extraordinary vitality of these poor wretches only prolonged their torments. So terrible were the sights and smells that the brain failed to realise the suffering and agony they proclaimed. As a man faints and his body refuses to suffer beyond a certain degree under torture, so the mind was unable to appreciate that an arrangement of line and colour lying on the ground was a human being, partly putrefied but still alive. Perhaps stern Nature, more merciful than stern civilisation, lent a kindly delirium. But I must record the fact that most of the men I saw

were sane and capable of feeling every pang. And meanwhile they
all struggled towards the Nile, the great river of their country,
without which the invaders could never have come upon them, but
which they nevertheless did not reproach. One man had reached it
and lay exhausted, but content, on the bank. Another had attained
the water and had died at its brim. Let us hope he had his drink
first.

All this was three days after the action. Yet on the 9th of September, when a week had passed, there were still a few wounded
who had neither died nor crawled away, but continued to suffer.
How had they lived? It is not possible that they could have existed
so long without food and water. The women and the disarmed
population of Omdurman had been busy. Many hundreds not quite
helpless had dragged themselves off and died all along the line of
retreat. Those who were from the country round Omdurman had
succour from their relations and neighbours; but it was bad for the
man who had come from far and had no friends. The women would
perhaps spare him a few drops of water—enough to help him
through the day—but if he were a stranger, they would do no more.

Thus it was that these painful and shocking cases occurred, and
it is not easy to see how they could have been prevented. The statement that 'the wounded Dervishes received every delicacy and attention' is so utterly devoid of truth that it transcends the limits
of mendacity and passes into the realms of the ridiculous. I was
impatient to get back to the camp. There was nothing to be gained
by dallying on the field, unless a man were anxious to become quite
callous, so that no imaginable misery which could come to human
flesh would ever have moved him again. I may have written in these
pages something of vengeance and of the paying of a debt. It may be
that vengeance is sweet, and that the gods forbade vengeance to
men because they reserved for themselves so delicious and intoxi-
cating a drink. But no one should drain the cup to the bottom. The
dregs are often filthy-tasting.

"THE DULL, DARK CLOUDS OF MILITARISM" [2]

*Almost as soon as Churchill had entered Parliament in
1900 he began to speak about major questions. Although he*

[2] From *Parliamentary Debates: House of Commons*, May 13, 1901. (Hereafter
referred to as *Hansard*.) *Hansard* provides the official record of debates in the

*was at this time a member of the Conservative Party, he did
not hesitate to criticize his own party and its leaders. One of
his most outspoken orations was against the proposed increase
in military expenditure. He was twenty-six at the time.*

The enormous and varied frontiers of the Empire, and our
many points of contact with barbarous peoples, will surely in the
future, as in the past, draw us into frequent little wars. Our military
system must therefore be adapted for dealing with these minor
emergencies smoothly and conveniently. But we must not expect
to meet the great civilised Powers in this easy fashion. We must not
regard war with a modern Power as a kind of game in which we
may take a hand, and with good luck and good management may
play adroitly for an evening and come safe home with our winnings. It is not that, and I rejoice that it cannot be that. A European war cannot be anything but a cruel, heartrending struggle,
which, if we are ever to enjoy the bitter fruits of victory, must
demand, perhaps for several years, the whole manhood of the
nation, the entire suspension of peaceful industries, and the con-
centrating to one end of every vital energy in the community. I
have frequently been astonished since I have been in this House
to hear with what composure and how glibly Members and even
Ministers, talk of a European war. I will not expatiate on the
horrors of war, but there has been a great change which the House
should not omit to notice. In former days, when wars arose from
individual causes, from the policy of a Minister or the passion of a
King, when they were fought by small regular armies of professional
soldiers, and when their course was retarded by the difficulties of
communication and supply, and often suspended by the winter sea-
son, it was possible to limit the liabilities of the combatants. But
now, when mighty populations are impelled on each other, each
individual severally embittered and inflamed—when the resources
of science and civilisation sweep away everything that might mitigate their fury, a European war can only end in the ruin of the
vanquished and the scarcely less fatal commercial dislocation and

House of Commons and House of Lords. Reprinted by permission of the Controller of Her Majesty's Stationery Office. Churchill's parliamentary speeches are
the finest single source for his life's activity. The majority of them have never
been reprinted in book form. For any episode in which he was involved, the
pages of *Hansard* deserve the fullest scrutiny.

exhaustion of the conquerors. Democracy is more vindictive than
Cabinets. The wars of peoples will be more terrible than those of
kings.

*   *   *

The armies of Europe are bigger than those of the Boers, and
cheaper than our own. France, in this present year, for an expenditure of twenty-eight millions, can mobilise twenty army corps. Germany, for twenty-six millions, gets twenty-two army corps. Russia,
for thirty-two millions, can set on foot, including twenty-three regular army corps, a total force estimated at over three millions of men.
And what can Great Britain do? Taught by the experience of the
South African War, rich in her commerce and the generosity of her
people, guided by the unfailing instinct of the War Office, Great
Britain would be defended, after this scheme has been carried into
effect, by no fewer than three trained army corps and three partly
trained army corps; and for this she must pay two millions a year
more than France, four millions a year more than Germany, and
within two millions of the total cost of the whole great Russian
army. But in spite of every explanatory circumstance, after every
allowance has been made, one great truth glows and glares in our
faces, veil it how we may: standing armies, which abound on the
European continent, are not indigenous to the British soil; they
do not flourish in our climate, they are not suited to our national
character, and though with artificial care and at a huge and dis-
proportionate cost we may cultivate and preserve them, they will
after all only be poor, stunted, sickly plants of foreign origin. The
Empire which has grown up around these islands is essentially commercial and marine. The whole course of our history, the geography
of the country, all the evidences of the present situation, proclaim
beyond a doubt that our power and prosperity alike and together
depend on the economic command of markets and the naval command of the sea; and from the highest sentimental reasons, not less
than from the most ordinary practical considerations, we must avoid
a servile imitation of the clanking military empires of the European
continent, by which we cannot obtain the military predominance
and security which is desired, but only impair and vitiate the natural sources of our strength and vigour. There is a higher reason
still. There is a moral force—the Divine foundation of earthly

power—which, as the human race advances, will more and more
strengthen and protect those who enjoy it; which would have protected the Boers better than all their cannon and brave commandos
if instead of being ignorant, aggressive, and corrupt, they had
enjoyed that high moral reputation which protected us in the dark
days of the war from European interference—for, in spite of every
calumny and lie uttered or printed, the truth comes to the top, and
it is known alike by peoples and by rulers that on the whole British
influence is healthy and kindly, and makes for the general happiness
and welfare of mankind. And we shall make a fatal bargain if we
allow the moral force which this country has so long exerted to become diminished, or perhaps even destroyed for the sake of the
costly, trumpery playthings on which the Secretary of State for War
has set his heart. . . .

But I will not sit down without urging on you something more
than counsels of expediency. Europe groans beneath the weight of
armies. There is scarcely a single important government whose
finances are not embarrassed; there is not a Parliament or a people
from whom the cry of weariness has not been wrung. The preparations of one State are followed by counter-preparations of its neigh-
bour. On all sides the millions have been squandered everywhere,
the armies have fattened on the impoverishment of nations, and the
dull dark clouds of militarism brood over the Continent, shutting
out the sunshine of prosperity and freedom in which the happier
peoples of Britain and the United States have so long thrived and
flourished. Now suddenly from the smoke and dust of the South
African War there has come a message full of hope; as it were a
promise that in proportion as Science is made to serve the purposes
of war it will become much easier for people to defend their own
lands, much harder for others to assail them. What a pity it would
be if, just at the moment when there is good hope of a change, our
statesmen were to commit us to the old and vicious policy! Is it not
a much more splendid dream that this realm of England—which
has formerly done much good service to mankind, which has secured
liberty to the slave, which compassed the downfall of Napoleon,
whose laws form the jurisprudence of the most enlightened States,
whose polity is the model and envy of the world—should be found
bold enough and strong enough to send forth on the wings of
honest purpose the message which the Russian Emperor tried vainly

to proclaim: that the cruel and clanking struggle of armaments is
drawing to a close, and that with the New Century has come a
clearer and a calmer sky.

ENGLAND ON THE EVE OF WAR [3]

*Churchill's fears in 1901 that a European war would be
neither short nor easy were amply justified by events. World
War I revealed in full measure the accuracy of his forebodings.
Over a million British and Dominion troops died in the holocaust. Looking back after 1918, Churchill realized how naïve
it had been for men to have assumed that because war would
clearly be so terrible, statesmen would therefore succeed in
avoiding it. Writing in 1923, Churchill pictured the general
state of mind in 1911, when the first war-clouds had sped fleet-
ingly across the European sky, but when Britain, Germany,
and France had been able to solve the crisis by diplomatic
exchanges.*

They sound so very cautious and correct, these deadly words.
Soft, quiet voices purring, courteous, grave, exactly-measured
phrases in large peaceful rooms. But with less warning, cannons had
opened fire and nations had been struck down by this same Germany. So now the Admiralty wireless whispers through the ether
to the tall masts of ships, and captains pace their decks absorbed
in thought. It is nothing. It is less than nothing. It is too foolish,
too fantastic to be thought of in the twentieth century. Or is it
fire and murder leaping out of the darkness at our throats, tor-
pedoes ripping the bellies of half-awakened ships, a sunrise on
a vanished naval supremacy, and an island well-guarded hitherto,
at last defenceless? No, it is nothing. No one would do such things.
Civilization has climbed above such perils. The interdependence of
nations in trade and traffic, the sense of public law, the Hague Convention, Liberal principles, the Labour Party, high finance, Christian charity, common sense have rendered such nightmares impossible. Are you quite sure? It would be a pity to be wrong. Such a mistake could only be made once—once for all.

[3] From Winston S. Churchill, *The World Crisis* (London, 1923), I, 48-49.
Reprinted by permission of Charles Scribner's Sons.

"WILL OUR CHILDREN BLEED AND GASP AGAIN?" [4]

Churchill's five-volume history of World War I, The World
Crisis, *which was published between 1923 and 1931, is full of
general comments on the ethics of war as well as being a detailed and richly documented narratives of events.*

The great War through which we have passed differed from
all ancient wars in the immense power of the combatants and their
fearful agencies of destruction, and from all modern wars in the
utter ruthlessness with which it was fought. All the horrors of all
the ages were brought together, and not only armies but whole
populations were thrust into the midst of them. The mighty educated States involved conceived with reason that their very existence
was at stake. Germany having let Hell loose kept well in the van
of terror; but she was followed step by step by the desperate and
ultimately avenging nations she had assailed. Every outrage against
humanity or international law was repaid by reprisals often on a
greater scale and of longer duration. No truce or parley mitigated
the strife of the armies. The wounded died between the lines: the
dead mouldered into the soil. Merchant ships and neutral ships and
hostile ships were sunk on the seas and all on board left to their fate,
or killed as they swam. Every effort was made to starve whole nations into submission without regard to age or sex. Cities and monuments were smashed by artillery. Bombs from the air were cast down
indiscriminately. Poison gas in many forms stifled or seared the soldiers. Liquid fire was projected upon their bodies. Men fell from
the air in flames, or were smothered, often slowly, in the dark
recesses of the sea. The fighting strength of armies was limited only
by the manhood of their countries. Europe and large parts of Asia
and Africa became one vast battlefield on which after years of
struggle not armies but nations broke and ran. When all was over,
Torture and Cannibalism were the only two expedients that the
civilized, scientific, Christian States had been able to deny themselves: and these were of doubtful utility.

But nothing daunted the valiant heart of man. Son of the Stone

[4] From Winston S. Churchill, *The World Crisis* (London, 1923-31), I, 10-11
and III, 544. Reprinted by permission of Charles Scribner's Sons.

Age, vanquisher of nature with all her trials and monsters, he met the awful and self-inflicted agony with new reserves of fortitude. Freed in the main by his intelligence from mediaeval fears, he marched to death with sombre dignity. His nervous system was found in the twentieth century capable of enduring physical and moral stresses before which the simpler natures of primeval times would have collapsed. Again and again to the hideous bombardment, again and again from the hospital to the front, again and again to the hungry submarines he strode unflinching. And withal, as an individual, preserved through these torments the glories of a reasonable and compassionate mind.

The curtain falls upon the long front in France and Flanders. The soothing hands of Time and Nature, the swift repair of peaceful industry, have already almost effaced the crater fields and the battle lines which in a broad belt from the Vosges to the sea lately blackened the smiling fields of France. The ruins are rebuilt, the riven trees are replaced by new plantations. Only the cemeteries, the monuments and stunted steeples, with here and there a mouldering trench or huge mine-crater lake, assail the traveller with the fact that twenty-five millions of soldiers fought here and twelve millions shed their blood or perished in the greatest of all human contentions less than ten years ago. Merciful oblivion draws its veils; the crippled limp away; the mourners fall back into the sad twilight of memory. New youth is here to claim its rights, and the perennial stream flows forward even in the battle zone, as if the tale were all a dream.

Is this the end? Is it to be merely a chapter in a cruel and senseless story? Will a new generation in their turn be immolated to square the black accounts of Teuton and Gaul? Will our children bleed and gasp again in devastated lands? Or will there spring from the very fires of conflict that reconciliation of the three giant combatants, which would unite their genius and secure to each in safety and freedom a share in rebuilding the glory of Europe?

"THE CLEAR PATH OF DUTY"

However much Churchill abhorred the strife of civilized nations locked in vile and destructive conflict, he never lost sight of the nobility of individual bravery. He saw clearly that

*whereas historians and politicians might argue over the rights
and wrongs of war for a long time, and seek to fix the blame
for any particular war on their opponents, the individual soldier acted from a simple sense of duty and without thought
of personal advancement. Churchill regarded patriotism as a
high and important virtue. He admired most those who responded to the call of duty when their nation was in danger.
In* The River War *he had shown this admiration not only
toward his own fellow soldiers but also toward the Sudanese
dervishes against whom he was fighting. Immediately after the
South African war he had spoken with equal sympathy and
understanding of the individual courage of the Boers. His
praise for individual acts of heroism was never limited to the
heroism of his own side. In 1925 at the unveiling of a memorial
to the dead of the Royal Naval Division he delivered the following speech which fully reflects his admiration for those who
died in the call of duty.*

Here under the shadow of the Admiralty building, where,
eleven years ago, the Royal Naval Division was called into martial
life, this monument now records their fame and preserves their
memory. Their memory is thus linked for ever with the Royal Navy,
whose child they were, of whose traditions they were so proud, and
whose long annals, rich with romantic and splendid feats of arms,
contains no brighter page than theirs. But if the place is well
chosen, so also is the day. This is April 25th, and ten years ago the
astonishing exploit of landing on the Gallipoli Peninsula was in full
battle. And we here, who have so many memories in common,
almost seem to hear the long reverberations of the distant cannon-
ade, and certainly we feel again in our souls the awful hopes and
awful fears of those tragic hours. . . .

We are often tempted to ask ourselves what we gained by the
enormous sacrifices made by those to whom this memorial is erected.
But this was never the issue with those who marched away. No
question of advantage presented itself to their minds. They only
saw the light shining on the clear path of duty. They only saw their
duty to resist oppression, to protect the weak, to vindicate the
profound but unwritten laws of nations, to testify to truth and
justice and mercy among men. They never asked the question,
'What shall we gain?' They asked only the question, 'Where lies
the right?' It was thus that they marched away for ever, and yet

from their uncalculating exaltation and devotion, detached from all consideration of material gain, we may be sure that good will come to their countrymen and to this island they guarded in its reputation and safety so faithfully and so well.[5]

Sixteen years later, in November 1941, Churchill wrote an introduction to the biography of a young Conservative Member of Parliament who had been killed during the retreat to Dunkirk. Again he showed his admiration for and appreciation of personal sacrifice in a national cause.

Ronald Cartland was a man of noble spirit, who followed his convictions without thought of personal advancement. At a time when our political life had become feckless and dull, he spoke fearlessly for Britain. His words and acts were instinct with the sense of our country's traditions and duty. His courage and bearing inspired those who met him or heard him.

Fortunately this country has not lacked men prepared to spend their lives in its service. Ronald Cartland was one of these. On 30 May 1940, when he was killed fighting with the rear guard of the British Expeditionary Force during its retreat to Dunkirk, the Army and the House of Commons suffered a grievous loss. Those who read this book will realize that this is true. They will also derive from it a renewed assurance that the way of life for which he fought will certainly prevail and persist because of the striving and sacrifices of such men as he.[6]

"IN WAR, RESOLUTION . . . IN PEACE, GOODWILL" [7]

In his memoirs, which like nearly all his books contained almost as much philosophical reflection as factual narrative,

---

[5] Quoted in Lord Justice Birkett, "Churchill the Orator," in Charles Eade, ed., *Churchill by His Contemporaries* (London, 1953), chap. 27, p. 228. Reprinted by permission of Miss Diana Eade and Charles Eade's Executor.

[6] Quoted in Barbara Cartland, *Ronald Cartland* (London, 1941), p. 15. Reprinted by permission of Miss Barbara Cartland. Ronald Cartland had distinguished himself during his short parliamentary career both by his pugnacious refusal to accept social inequalities and by his hostility to the policy of appeasing Nazi Germany.

[7] From Winston S. Churchill, *My Early Life* (London, 1931), p. 346. Quoted by permission of Charles Scribner's Sons.

Churchill analyzed his own attitude toward war. He had formed these opinions as a young man and sustained them throughout his life. Nor did the experience of two major world wars alter his basic view that threatened nations should seek to defend themselves, that nations at war should fight with all the courage and sacrifice at their command, and that once wars were ended the victorious powers should turn their sympathy toward those they had defeated and should seek to build on the basis of reconciliation of a new international structure freed from bitterness.

I have always urged fighting wars and other contentions with might and main till overwhelming victory, and then offering the hand of friendship to the vanquished. Thus, I have always been against the Pacifists during the quarrel, and against the Jingoes at its close. Many years after this South African incident, Lord Birkenhead mentioned to me a Latin quotation which seems to embody this idea extremely well. *Parcere subjectis et debellare superbos,* which he translated finely, "Spare the conquered and war down the proud." I seem to have come very near achieving this thought by my own untutored reflections. . . .

I was once asked to devise an inscription for a monument in France. I wrote, 'In war, Resolution; in defeat, Defiance; in victory, Magnanimity; in peace, Goodwill.' The inscription was not accepted. It is all the fault of the human brain being made in two lobes, only one of which does any thinking, so that we are all right-handed or left-handed; whereas, if we were properly constructed, we should use our right and left hands with equal force and skill according to circumstances. As it is, those who can win a war well can rarely make a good peace, and those who could make a good peace would never have won the war. It would perhaps be pressing the argument too far to suggest that I could do both.

2

Government and Reform

Democracy is not a caucus, obtaining a fixed term of office by promises and then doing what it likes with the people. Government of the people, by the people, for the people, still remains the sovereign definition of democracy.

—CHURCHILL

Churchill entered Parliament in order to get things done. From the age of twenty-six he played a leading part in urging upon successive British Governments a comprehensive policy of social reform. In this chapter are extracts from a number of his speeches in which he expressed his profound belief in parliamentary democracy, and in a blend of private enterprise and State action which he considered the ideal combination for striking at social injustice.

THE NEW ROLE OF THE STATE [1]

Churchill explained his basic social philosophy, and the objectives which he felt were within the immediate grasp of Government, in a speech which he delivered in Glasgow in October 1906.

It is not possible to draw a hard-and-fast line between individualism and collectivism. You cannot draw it either in theory or in practice. That is where the Socialist makes a mistake. Let us not imitate that mistake. No man can be a collectivist alone or an individualist alone. He must be both an individualist and

[1] Quoted in Winston S. Churchill, *Liberalism and the Social Problem* (London, 1909), pp. 79-83, 315-17. Reprinted by permission of Odhams Press Limited, proprietors of the copyright. The reader should also consult Churchill's other volume on the social question, *The People's Rights* (London, 1910).

a collectivist. The nature of man is a dual nature. The character of the organisation of human society is dual. Man is at once a unique being and a gregarious animal. For some purposes he must be collectivist, for others he is, and he will for all time remain, an individualist. Collectively we have an Army and a Navy and a Civil Service; collectively we have a Post Office, and a police, and a Government; collectively we light our streets and supply ourselves with water; collectively we indulge increasingly in all the necessities of communication. But we do not make love collectively, and the ladies do not marry us collectively, and we do not eat collectively, and we do not die collectively, and it is not collectively that we face the sorrows and the hopes, the winnings and the losings of this world of accident and storm.

No view of society can possibly be complete which does not comprise within its scope both collective organisation and individual incentive. The whole tendency of civilisation is, however, towards the multiplication of the collective functions of society. The ever-growing complications of civilisation create for us new services which have to be undertaken by the State, and create for us an expansion of the existing services. There is a growing feeling, which I entirely share, against allowing those services which are in the nature of monopolies to pass into private hands. There is a pretty steady determination, which I am convinced will become effective in the present Parliament, to intercept all future unearned increment which may arise from the increase in the speculative value of the land. There will be an ever-widening area of municipal enterprise. I go farther; I should like to see the State embark on various novel and adventurous experiments. I am delighted to see that Mr. Burns is now interesting himself in afforestation. I am of opinion that the State should increasingly assume the position of the reserve employer of labour. I am very sorry we have not got the railways of this country in our hands. We may do something better with the canals, and we are all agreed, every one in this hall who belongs to the Progressive Party, that the State must increasingly and earnestly concern itself with the care of the sick and the aged, and, above all, of the children.

I look forward to the universal establishment of minimum standards of life and labour, and their progressive elevation as the increasing energies of production may permit. I do not think that

Liberalism in any circumstances can cut itself off from this fertile field of social effort, and I would recommend you not to be scared in discussing any of these proposals, just because some old woman comes along and tells you they are Socialistic. If you take my advice, you will judge each case on its merits. Where you find that State enterprise is likely to be ineffective, then utilise private enterprises, and do not grudge them their profits.

The existing organisation of society is driven by one mainspring —competitive selection. It may be a very imperfect organisation of society, but it is all we have got between us and barbarism. It is all we have been able to create through unnumbered centuries of effort and sacrifice. It is the whole treasure which past generations have been able to secure, and which they have been able to bequeath; and great and numerous as are the evils of the existing condition of society in this country, the advantages and achievements of the social system are greater still. Moreover, that system is one which offers an almost indefinite capacity for improvement. We may progressively eliminate the evils; we may progressively augment the goods which it contains. I do not want to see impaired the vigour of competition, but we can do much to mitigate the consequences of failure. We want to draw a line below which we will not allow persons to live and labour, yet above which they may compete with all the strength of their manhood. We want to have free competition upwards; we decline to allow free competition to run downwards. We do not want to pull down the structures of science and civilisation: but to spread a net over the abyss; and I am sure that if the vision of a fair Utopia which cheers the hearts and lights the imagination of the toiling multitudes, should ever break into reality, it will be by developments through, and modifications in, and by improvements out of, the existing competitive organisation of society; and I believe that Liberalism mobilised, and active as it is to-day, will be a principal and indispensable factor in that noble evolution.

At Manchester in May 1909 Churchill said:

The decisive question is this—will the British working classes embrace the opportunities which will shortly be offered to them? They are a new departure; they involve an element of compulsion and of regulation which is unusual in our happy-go-lucky English life. The opportunity may never return. For my own part, I confess to you, my friends in Manchester, that I would work for such a policy and would try to carry it through even if it were a little unpopular at first, and would be willing to pay the forfeit of a period of exclusion from power, in order to have carried such a policy through; because I know that there is no other way within the reach of this generation of men and women by which the stream of preventable misery can be cut off.

If I had my way I would write the word "Insure" over the door of every cottage, and upon the blotting-book of every public man, because I am convinced that by sacrifices which are inconceivably small, which are all within the power of the very poorest man in regular work, families can be secured against catastrophes which otherwise would smash them up for ever. I think it is our duty to use the strength and the resources of the State to arrest the ghastly waste not merely of human happiness but of national health and strength which follows when a working man's home which has taken him years to get together is broken up and scattered through a long spell of unemployment, or when, through the death, the sickness, or the invalidity of the bread-winner, the frail boat in which the fortunes of the family are embarked founders, and the women and children are left to struggle helplessly on the dark waters of a friendless world. I believe it is well within our power now, before this Parliament is over, to establish vast and broad throughout the land a mighty system of national insurance which will nourish in its bosom all worthy existing agencies and will embrace in its scope all sorts and conditions of men.

I think it is not untrue to say that in these years we are passing through a decisive period in the history of our country. The wonderful century which followed the Battle of Waterloo and the downfall of the Napoleonic domination, which secured to this small island so long and so resplendent a reign, has come to an end. We have arrived at a new time. Let us realise it. And with that new time strange methods, huge forces, larger combinations—a Titanic world—have sprung up around us. The foundations of our power are changing. To stand still would be to fall; to fall would be to perish. We must go forward. We will go forward. We will go forward into a way of life more earnestly viewed, more scientifically organised, more consciously national than any we have known. Thus alone shall we be able to sustain and to renew through the generations which are to come, the fame and the power of the British race.

"THE UNNATURAL GAP BETWEEN RICH AND POOR" [2]

Speaking at Leicester in 1909 Churchill explained what he considered the greatest danger to Britain at that time.

The greatest danger to the British empire and to the British people is not to be found among the enormous fleets and armies of the European Continent, nor in the solemn problems of Hindustan; it is not the Yellow peril nor the Black peril nor any danger in the wide circuit of colonial and foreign affairs. No, it is here in our midst, close at home, close at hand in the vast growing cities of England and Scotland, and in the dwindling and cramped villages of our denuded countryside. It is there you will find the seeds of Imperial ruin and national decay—the unnatural gap between rich and poor, the divorce of the people from the land, the want of proper discipline and training in our youth, the exploitation of boy labour, the physical degeneration which seems to follow so swiftly on civilised poverty, the awful jumbles of an obsolete Poor Law, the horrid havoc of the liquor traffic, the constant insecurity in the means of subsistence and employment which breaks the heart of many a sober, hard-working man, the absence of any established minimum standard of life and comfort among the workers, and, at the other end, the swift increase of vulgar, joyless luxury—here are the enemies of Britain. Beware lest they shatter the foundations of her power.

Then look at the other side, look at the forces for good, the moral forces, the spiritual forces, the civic, the scientific, the patriotic forces which make for order and harmony and health and life. Are they not tremendous too? Do we not see them everywhere, in every town, in every class, in every creed, strong forces worthy of Old England, coming to her rescue, fighting for her soul? That is the

[2] Quoted in Winston S. Churchill, *Liberalism and the Social Problem* (London, 1909), pp. 363-64. Reprinted by permission of Odhams Press Limited, proprietors of the copyright.

situation in our country as I see it this afternoon—two great armies evenly matched, locked in fierce conflict with each other all along the line, swaying backwards and forwards in strife—and for my part I am confident that the right will win, that the generous influences will triumph over the selfish influences, that the organising forces will devour the forces of degeneration, and that the British people will emerge triumphant from their struggles to clear the road and lead the march amongst the foremost nations of the world.

ATTACKING THE HOUSE OF LORDS [3]

The serious barrier to social reform before World War I was the power of the House of Lords to reject legislation proposed by the House of Commons. The whole liberal progress with which Churchill was so closely associated both as a legislator and as a public speaker was threatened by the unrelenting hostility of the House of Lords. The Liberal Government therefore took action under the Parliament Act of 1911 which destroyed the veto powers of the House of Lords and thereby swept away the final barrier to radical social change in Britain. Despite the fact that he was a grandson of a Duke, Churchill was among the most vigorous opponents of the House of Lords. He had no sympathy whatsoever for power based solely and irresponsibly upon privilege and heredity. His public attacks on the House of Lords were direct, dramatic, and—for the House of Lords—disastrous.

Is it not an extraordinary thing that upon the Budget we should even be discussing at all the action of the House of Lords? The House of Lords is an institution absolutely foreign to the spirit of the age and to the whole movement of society. It is not perhaps surprising in a country so fond of tradition, so proud of continuity, as ourselves that a feudal assembly of titled persons, with so long a history and so many famous names, should have survived to exert an influence upon public affairs at the present time. We see how often in England the old forms are reverently

[3] Quoted in Winston S. Churchill, *Liberalism and the Social Problem* (London, 1909), pp. 352-53. Reprinted by permission of Odhams Press Limited, proprietors of the copyright.

preserved long after the forces by which they were sustained and the uses to which they were put and the dangers against which they were designed have passed away. A state of gradual decline was what the average Englishman had come to associate with the House of Lords. Little by little, we might have expected, it would have ceased to take a controversial part in practical politics. Year by year it would have faded more completely into the past to which it belongs until, like Jack-in-the-Green or Punch-and-Judy, only a picturesque and fitfully lingering memory would have remained.

And during the last ten years of Conservative government this was actually the case. But now we see the House of Lords flushed with the wealth of the modern age, armed with a party caucus, fortified, revived, resuscitated, asserting its claims in the harshest and in the crudest manner, claiming to veto or destroy even without discussion any legislation, however important, sent to them by any majority, however large, from any House of Commons, however newly elected. We see these unconscionable claims exercised with a frank and undisguised regard to party interest, to class interest, and to personal interest. We see the House of Lords using the power which they should not hold at all, which if they hold at all, they should hold in trust for all, to play a shrewd, fierce, aggressive party game of electioneering and casting their votes according to the interest of the particular political party to which, body and soul, they belong.

Sometimes Churchill's tone was less brutish:

These unfortunate individuals who ought to lead quiet, delicate, sheltered lives, far from the madding crowd's ignoble strife, have been dragged into the football scrimmage, and they have got rather roughly mauled in the process. . . . Do not let us be too hard on them. It is poor sport—almost like teasing goldfish. These ornamental creatures blunder on every hook they see, and there is no sport whatever in trying to catch them. It would be barbarous to leave them gasping upon the bank of public ridicule upon which they have landed themselves. Let us put them back gently, tenderly in their fountains; and if a few bright scales have been rubbed off in what the Prime Minister calls the variegated handling they have received, they will soon get over it. They have got plenty more.

TONYPANDY [4]

The social reform of Asquith's Liberal Government was not enough to quell the deep social discontent; unrest grew, culminating in strikes and riots. Churchill was in a dilemma. He wished to continue social legislation, but he opposed the destructive methods of the extremists among the strikers. The State had a duty, he believed, to protect the citizen and his property against anarchic violence. Nevertheless, Churchill opposed the use of military force by the State except in times of the utmost danger to civilian life and property. Such moments were rare; but 1910 saw one of them in the form of violent action, looting, and hooliganism by men on strike. The local authorities demanded instant military support, and called soldiers from London. But Churchill was still not convinced that they were necessary, although later, during the Liverpool riots, he saw the need for them. He at once halted the train with the soldiers in it, and replaced them by unarmed London policemen, who succeeded in stopping the mob violence. He was immediately attacked in Parliament by the Conservatives for undue leniency. His reply reveals his deep respect for moderate Government.

Law and order must be preserved, but I am confident that the House will agree with me that it is a great object of public policy to avoid a collision between soldiers and crowds of persons engaged in industrial disputes. . . . For soldiers to fire on the people would be a catastrophe in our national life. Alone among the nations, or almost alone, we have avoided for a great many years that melancholy and unnatural experience. And it is well worth while, I venture to think, for the Minister who is responsible to run some risk of broken heads or broken windows . . . to accept

---

[4] *Hansard,* February 7, 1911. Reprinted by permission of the Controller of Her Majesty's Stationery Office. For a comprehensive account of the "Tonypandy" incident, and of Churchill's reluctance to use armed force, see Sir Alan Herbert, "Winston and the Workers" published in the London *Spectator,* June 28, 1963. Churchill was not unsympathetic to the strikers, whom he considered had been "hardly tried in more ways than one," and he warned the mine-owners not to consider police or military forces as "their private lackeys and flunkeys." In August 1911 he reiterated that "There can be no question of the military forces of the Crown intervening in a labour dispute," see Peter de Mendelssohn, *The Age of Churchill* (London, 1961), pp. 494-98.

direct responsibility in order that the shedding of British blood by British soldiers may be averted, as, thank God, it has been successfully averted in South Wales.

THE FOUNDATIONS OF DEMOCRACY [5]

Churchill never forgot the vital importance of parliamentary democracy. Indeed, in two World Wars he played a major part in enabling democratic government to survive the attacks of aggressive and dictatorial states. In October 1944, and again in November 1950, Churchill reminded Parliament of the essential tenets of democracy as he saw them.

The foundation of all democracy is that the people have the right to vote. To deprive them of that right is to make a mockery of all the high-sounding phrases which are so often used. At the bottom of all the tributes paid to democracy is the little man, walking into the little booth, with a little pencil, making a little cross on a little bit of paper—no amount of rhetoric or voluminous discussion can possibly diminish the overwhelming importance of that point.

Six years later Churchill re-iterated:

We must not forget what votes are. Votes are the means by which the poorest people in the country and all people in the country can make sure that they get their vital needs attended to.

[5] From *Hansard,* October 31, 1944, and November 6, 1950. Reprinted by permission of the Controller of Her Majesty's Stationery Office.

3
Empire

*I have a tendency, against which I should, perhaps, be
on my guard, to swim against the stream. At all times,
according to my mights and throughout the changing
scenes through which we are all hurried, I have always
faithfully served two public causes which, I think,
stand supreme—the maintenance of the enduring greatness of Britain and her Empire and the historic continuity of our island life.*

—CHURCHILL

Churchill was never an Imperialist in the aggressive sense of seeking to conquer new territories over which
to extend British dominion. What he believed in tenaciously
throughout his political career was that Britain held a responsibility to her Imperial possessions, not only to maintain law
and order, but also to enhance the prosperity of her subjects,
whatever the color of their skins. His great hope was that all
such progress would take place under British sovereignty. He
was therefore much disappointed when the rapid rise of nationalism between the wars led to a demand, particularly in
India, for the end of British rule. The Indian Nationalists
believed that Britain should give up her Empire as soon as
possible. Churchill wanted Britain to maintain the Empire
and to show that under British guidance prosperity and progress could be ensured. He did not believe that the nationalist
Congress Party could be as effective and as beneficent as British
rule. Churchill underrated the power of nationalism to turn
people against every aspect, however beneficial, of Imperial
rule. In the 1930s his anger was fierce against those who challenged the power of Britain to rule effectively, but when the
Labour Government granted India full independence in 1947
Churchill spoke of the need for sympathy with the Indian
people.

CONSTRUCTIVE IMPERIALISM

The following three passages show Churchill searching for a constructive Imperialism—firstly, during the immediate aftermath of the war in the Sudan when he had fought to reinstate British rule; secondly, when he had moved from the Conservative Party to the Liberal Party in 1904; and thirdly, in conversation with a strong critic of British Imperial rule in 1909.

The course to be pursued steadily, deliberately, and prudently, is clear. First of all, to establish law and order in the Soudan; then to borrow money, with the help of Egypt, on easy terms for the building of a barrage and subsidiary canals to provide for the winter irrigation of the Blue Nile basin; with the increase of wealth which shall gradually accrue from this investment, and aided by the growing resources of Egypt, to stop the leakage of the White Nile. The increase of water thus obtained by Egypt will render it possible to provide for the summer irrigation of the Blue Nile basin; the increase of wealth resulting from the increase of water may enable Egypt to assist with capital; and these gigantic enterprises may in their turn prove but the preliminaries of even mightier schemes, until at last nearly every drop of water which drains into the whole valley of the Nile, preserved from evaporation or discharge, shall be equally and amicably divided among the river-peoples—and the Nile itself, flowing for three thousand miles through smiling countries, shall perish gloriously and never reach the sea.[1]

Four years later Churchill said:

Mr. Chamberlain has said that this is a day of great empires and not of small states. I do not admit that proposition. Empires which are great only in the sense of being large, which are mere agglomerations of reluctant people shackled together by a central Government and an army, such empires have often in the past collapsed, and will often again collapse before the onslaught of a

[1] From Winston S. Churchill, *The River War* (London, 1900), II, 411. Reprinted by permission of Odhams Press Limited, proprietors of the copyright. For Churchill's constructive views on Empire see also his book *My African Journey* (London, 1908), published when he was Under-Secretary of State for the Colonies.

small homogeneous people actuated by an intenser form of patriotic sentiment. If 'that defensive league of communities under the august headship of the English Crown', as Lord Rosebery has finely termed the British Empire—if that league be found to possess the qualities which endure the changes and shocks of the centuries, it will not be because the British Empire possesses more square miles of territory than the Empire of Russia; it will not be because it owns more subjects than the Empire of China; it will not be because it is guarded by more soldiers than the Empire of Germany: it will be because it is based upon the assent of free peoples, united with each other by noble and progressive principles; because it is animated by respect of right and justice in its dealings, whether great or small, with the nations; and because in the future history of the world, as in the past, it shall be found, on the whole, to be an agent of human progress and of international peace.[2]

Shortly after Churchill entered the Cabinet the controversial publicist and radical Wilfrid Scawen Blunt recorded:

Winston sympathizes much with my ideas about the native question in India, and in general about the enslavement of the coloured by the white race. But he says he is an Imperialist, and his chief interest is in the condition and welfare of the poor in England, who, he says, are far worse off than the poor in any part of the East. 'I would give my life,' he said, 'to see them placed on a right footing in regard to their lives and means of living. That is what I am paid for, and I would really give my life.' I can see all the same that my arguments have effect on him, just as they used to have with his father; and I should not be surprised if some day he made the Indian cause his own. . . .

In the evening we had another great discussion of the fundamentals of politics, each of us holding our own ground. Mine was, of course, that of 'Satan Absolved,' to which Winston opposed one of optimistic Liberal Imperialism where the British Empire was to be maintained, in part by concession, in part by force, and the constant invention of new scientific forces to deal with growing

[2] From a speech delivered at the Cobden Centenary Dinner in Manchester on June 3, 1904, and widely reported in the newspapers at the time. Quoted in A. MacCallum Scott, *Winston Spencer Churchill* (London, 1905), pp. 258-59.

difficulties of Imperial rule. He admitted, however, that India does not pay its expense to us in men or money; and it seems to me that he would be pretty easily persuaded to let it go, were the pressure severe enough. Like most of them, it is the vanity of Empire that affects him more than supposed profit or the necessities of trade, which he repudiates; also, doubtless, his military training counts for much in his Imperialism. He will come round to me in time.[8]

BRITISH RIGHTS IN INDIA [4]

So fiercely did Churchill challenge the Conservative policy of eventual self-government for India—a policy advocated by the Conservative leader Stanley Baldwin in 1931—that he found himself rejected by the Conservatives whose ranks he had rejoined only a few years before in 1924. He published his speeches in opposition to this policy in a volume, India, *in 1931. Extracts from his speech in Parliament in January of that same year showed clearly the strength of his feelings.*

The clash and agitation in India will continue, but they will no longer be confined to rioting in the streets or demonstrations in the Legislature. They will invade the heart and the brain of the Government of India. There, at the summit of this wonderful creation, an instrument which, with all its shortcomings, has given peace and progress to nations more varied than the nations of Europe and populations in the aggregate almost as large as China —there, at the summit, by constitutional and Parliamentary weapons now, the process of gnawing and cutting down the safeguards will proceed, stimulated, perhaps, from outside by a continuance of lawlessness and rioting and of worse crimes, for the prevention of which you will no longer have the primary responsibility. What, may I ask, will be your line of moral and logical resistance then? You have declared that the safeguards are only transitory, they are

[8] From Wilfrid Scawen Blunt, *My Diaries, 1888-1914* (London, 1919-20), II, 690-91 (entry during 1909). Reprinted by permission of the Syndics of the Fitzwilliam Museum, Cambridge, England.

[4] *Hansard,* January 26, 1931. Reprinted by permission of the Controller of Her Majesty's Stationery Office. The speech is printed also in Winston Churchill, *India* (London, 1931), pp. 49-69.

temporary expedients, apologetically adopted pending, what (to anyone who reads this Blue Book, and notes the emphasis assigned to its various parts), can only mean the rapid and speedy realisation of full Dominion status. The struggle will go on; it will only be aggravated; it will proceed under conditions in which British rule will be shorn of all its argument and of half its apparatus. It will proceed steadily towards the goal which those who are driving this policy forward, both here in this country and in India, no longer hesitate to avow, namely, the goal of complete severance between Great Britain and India of every tie except tradition, which in India is adverse, and sentiment, which in India is hostile. Sir, I say that is a frightful prospect to have opened up so wantonly, so recklessly, so incontinently and in so short a time.

How will the British nation feel about this? I am told that they do not care. I am told that from one quarter or another. They are all worried by unemployment or taxation or absorbed in sport and crime news. The great liner is sinking in a calm sea. One bulkhead after another gives way; one compartment after another is bilged; the list increases; she is sinking; but the captain and the officers and the crew are all in the saloon dancing to the jazz band. But wait till the passengers find out what is their position! For thirty years I have watched from a central position the manifestations of the will power of Great Britain, and I do not believe our people will consent to be edged, pushed, talked and cozened out of India. No nation of which I am aware, great or small, has ever voluntarily or tamely suffered such an overwhelming injury to its interests or such a harsh abrogation of its rights. After all, there are British rights and interests in India. Two centuries of effort and achievement, lives given on a hundred fields, far more lives given and consumed in faithful and devoted service to the Indian people themselves! All this has earned us rights of our own in India. When the nation finds that our whole position is in jeopardy, that her whole work and duty in India is being brought to a standstill, when the nation sees our individual fellow-countrymen scattered about, with their women and children, throughout this enormous land, in hourly peril amidst the Indian multitudes, when, at any moment, this may produce shocking scenes, then I think there will be a sharp awakening, then, I am sure, that a reaction of the most vehement character will sweep this country and its unmeasured strength will once more be used. That, Sir, is an ending which I trust and pray we may avoid, but it is an ending to which, step by step and day by day, we are being remorselessly and fatuously conducted.

"THE CLATTERING DOWN OF THE BRITISH EMPIRE [5]

The first extract, from May 1947, reveals the depth of his sorrow and anger; the second, from October 1948, gives a clear indication of his willingness not only to accept a situation which he had no power to alter but also to welcome it and seek to draw hope from disappointment. Churchill was then leader of the Conservative Opposition in Parliament.

It is with deep grief I watch the clattering down of the British Empire with all its glories, and all the services it has rendered to mankind. I am sure that in the hour of our victory, now not so long ago, we had the power to make a solution of our difficulties which would have been honorable and lasting. Many have defended Britain against her foes. None can defend her against herself. We must face the evils that are coming upon us and that we are powerless to avert. We must do our best in these circumstances, and not exclude any expedient that may help to mitigate the ruin and disaster that will follow the disappearance of Britain from the East. But, at least, let us not add—by shameful flight, by a premature hurried scuttle—at least, let us not add to the pangs of sorrow so many of us feel, the taint and smear of shame.

A year and a half later Churchill said:

Our Imperial mission in India is at an end—we must recognise that. Some day justice will be done by world opinion to our record there, but the chapter is closed. . . .

We must look forward. It is our duty, whatever part we have taken in the past, to hope and pray for the well-being and happiness of all the peoples of India, of whatever race, religion, social condition or historic character they may be. We must wish them all well and do what we can to help them on their road. Sorrow

[5] From *Hansard,* March 6, 1947, and October 28, 1948. Reprinted by permission of the Controller of Her Majesty's Stationery Office.

may lie in our hearts but bitterness and malice must be purged from them, and in our future more remote relations with India we must rise above all prejudice and partiality—and not allow our vision to be clouded by memories of glories that are gone for ever. And in this temper we shall find true guidance—and, indeed, our only hope—in strict and faithful adherence to the underlying principles of justice and freedom which are embodied in the United Nations organisation, and for the maintenance of which that instrument of world government was consciously created.

It is those principles, and those principles alone, which must govern our attitude and action towards this vast branch of toiling and suffering humanity. We have long had no interest in India which counted for more with us than the well-being and peace of its peoples. So far as we may be involved in the fortunes of the Indian peoples, and of the Governments of Pakistan and Hindustan, we must judge them, not by race or religion, but impartially, by their future conduct to one another in accordance with the principles of the United Nations organisation under the Charter of human liberties which is being drawn up, and we must use our influence, such as it may be, against aggression, oppression and tyranny, from whatever quarter it comes. These principles alone must rule our actions, must enable us to steer our course in the incalculable tides on which we and our Indian fellow subjects are now embarked.

4

World Affairs

Appeasement from weakness and fear is alike futile
and fatal. Appeasement from strength is magnanimous
and noble, and might be the surest and perhaps the
only path to world peace.
                    —CHURCHILL (*During the Korean War*)

NO CAUSE FOR WAR [1]

Churchill was never a pacifist, but he believed that if na-
tions were sufficiently armed to defend themselves, then peace,
the pacifist's dream, could become a universal reality.

Before 1914, he hoped that war between civilized states
would be averted by common sense. He could see no cause
for quarrel so deep that it need plunge wealthy nations into
a mutually destructive and exhaustive conflict.

What about the 100 millions of people who dwell in these
islands and Germany? Are we all such sheep? Is democracy in the
20th century so powerless to effect its will? Are we all become such
puppets and marionettes to be wire-pulled against our interests into
such hideous convulsions? I have a high and prevailing faith in
the essential goodness of great people. I believe that working classes
all over the world are recognising they have common interests and
not divergent interests. I believe that what is called the international solidarity of labour has an immense boon to confer upon
all the peoples of the world. I was reading the other day of a story
in the war between Germany and France in 1870. The Germans
were occupying part of the French territory, and a visitor saw the

[1] From a speech delivered at Swansea on August 17, 1908, and widely reported
in the newspapers at the time. For Churchill's efforts to reduce naval armaments expenditure and to halt the naval arms-race before 1914, see his speech
in the House of Commons, March 26, 1913, published as *On Naval Armaments*
by the American Association for International Conciliation (New York, 1913).

German soldiers, who were of the hostile garrison, when not on duty, working in the fields by the side of French peasants helping them to get in their crops. One of the German soldiers was asked, 'Why do you do that to your enemy?' Said the German, 'War is all very well for the swells, but poor people have to help one another.' I have come here this afternoon to ask you to join with me in saying that far and wide throughout the masses of the British dominions there is no feeling of ill-will towards Germany. I say we honour that strong, patient industrious German people, who have been for so many centuries, a prey to European intrigue and a drudge amongst the nations of the Continent. Now in the fulness of time, after many tribulations, they have by their virtues and valour won themselves a foremost place in the front of civilization. I say we do not envy them their good fortune; we do not envy them their power and their prosperity. We are not jealous of them. We rejoice in everything that brings them good; we wish them well from the bottom of our heart, and we believe most firmly the victories they will win in science and learning against barbarism, against waste, the victories they will gain will be victories in which we shall share, and which, while benefiting them, will also benefit us.

. . . There is no collision of primary interests—big, important interests—between Great Britain and Germany in any quarter of the globe. Why, they are among our very best customers, and, if anything were to happen to them, I don't know what we should do in this country for a market. While there is no danger of a collision of material interests, there is no result which could be expected from any struggle between the two countries except a destruction of a most appalling and idiotic character. People said it would be well worth their fighting for the sake of our trade. Gentlemen, it is never worth while fighting for the sake of trade. In a month of fighting you would destroy more wealth than the successful trade of five years would produce if every one worked 12 hours a day. We are told there are colonies which could be seized by Germany. Why nothing will alter the destiny of great communities like Canada, Australia, South Africa, and India. They are pruning their own path and their own destiny, and that destiny will not be altered in the future as a result of any struggle between European powers. What remains as a prize to be fought for by two great countries? Nothing but tropical plantations and small coaling places scattered here and there about the world. Look at it from any point of view you like, and I say you will come to this conclusion in regard to the relations between England and Germany, that there is no real cause of difference between them, although there may be snapping and snarling in the newspapers and in the London clubs.

"REPAIR THE WASTE. REBUILD THE RUINS" [2]

In his writings after 1918 Churchill frequently warned the nations not to forget the horrors which they had seen and suffered during the war. He pleaded for a new approach to world problems which would not consider war making as the ultimate political maneuver, or as a mere incident in international life to be embarked upon with no less concern than upon a conference or a speech.

Why should war be the only purpose capable of uniting us in comradeship? Why should war be the only cause large enough to call forth really great and fine sacrifices? Look at the wonderful superb things people will do to carry on a war and to win a victory. Look what they will give up. Look what toils they achieve—what risks, what sufferings, what marvellous ingenuity, and what heroic and splendid qualities they display. All for war. Nothing is too good for war. Why cannot we have some of it for peace? Why is war to have all the splendours, all the nobleness, all the courage and loyalty? Why should peace have nothing but the squabbles and the selfishness and the pettiness of daily life? Why if men and women, all classes, all parties, are able to work together for five years like a mighty machine to produce *destruction*, can they not work together for another five years to produce *abundance?* All the arts and science that we used in war are standing by us now ready to help us in peace. All the organised power which moved the fleets and armies, which hunted the submarines in the depths of the sea, which made us the victors in the air, which produced unlimited munitions of

[2] From a speech delivered in November 1918, a few days after the armistice, and widely reported in the newspapers at the time. For Churchill's leading role in opposing harsh peace terms, and in urging Anglo-German reconciliation in the 1920s, see Martin Gilbert, *The Roots of Appeasement* (New York, 1966).

every intricate kind—all the clever brains, true brave hearts, strong unwearied hands—all are available. Only one thing do we require —a common principle of action, a plain objective, that everyone can understand and work for, as he worked to beat the German. Without this we cannot succeed. But surely we have a common purpose? Surely this period of reconstruction may be looked upon as if it were a part of the war? Surely if the sense of self-preservation enabled us to combine to conquer the same sense of self-preservation should enable us to restore and revive our prosperity? See how serious is the position. We have an enormous load of debt, far more than we shall ever get out of the Germans; capital is scarce and credit strained. The cost of living has risen to an unusual pitch, not only food, but boots and clothing, every necessity is scarce and costly. Our industries have all been distorted to war. They have to be turned back to peace. Railways, factories, housing—all have been neglected. Hundreds of thousands of men and women have got to change their employment and find a new job. On top of all this, we have to bring our soldiers home and make homes worthy for them and worthy of the deeds they have done. Surely this is a large enough task to satisfy us? Surely it is a sufficiently dangerous emergency to bring us altogether, to command loyal comradeship, to draw forth the inexhaustible treasures of the human heart? And, we can do it if we try. It will not be so hard as what we have already done, not half so hard. Five years of concerted effort by all classes, like what we have given in the war, but without its tragedies, would create an abundance and prosperity in this land, aye, throughout the world, such as has never yet been known or dreamt of. Five years of faction, of bickering, of class jealousies and Party froth, will not merely not give us prosperity; it will land us in utter and universal privation. The choice is in our own hands. Like the Israelites of old, blessing and cursing is set before us. To-day we can have the greatest failures or the greatest triumph—as we choose. There is enough for all. The earth is a generous mother. Never, never did science offer such fairy gifts to man. Never did their knowledge and organisation stand so high. Repair the waste. Rebuild the ruins. Heal the wounds. Crown the victors. Comfort the broken and broken-hearted. There is the battle we have now to fight. There is the victory we have now to win. Let us go forward together.

"DEATH STANDS AT ATTENTION" [3]

The origins and course of World War I impressed on Churchill the need to enlarge his ideas about world affairs. He still believed that the true object of all statesmanship should be the preservation of peace. But he now saw clearly that it was not enough for individual nations to be well armed for their own defense. It became his firm belief by 1935 that aggression could only be prevented, or if necessary checked, when nations who believed in the democratic way of life grouped themselves together in a defensive alliance. Only thus, he felt, would potential aggressors see, well in advance, the risks which they would take if they dared to trample upon the rights of their neighbors.

The campaign of 1919 was never fought; but its ideas go marching along. In every Army they are being explored, elaborated, refined under the surface of peace, and should war come again to the world it is not with the weapons and agencies prepared for 1919 that it will be fought, but with developments and extensions of these which will be incomparably more formidable and fatal.

It is in these circumstances that we have entered upon that period of Exhaustion which has been described as Peace. It gives us at any rate an opportunity to consider the general situation. Certain sombre facts emerge solid, inexorable, like the shapes of mountains from drifting mist. It is established that henceforward whole populations will take part in war, all doing their utmost, all subjected to the fury of the enemy. It is established that nations who believe their life is at stake will not be restrained from using any means to secure their existence. It is probable—nay, certain—that among the means which will next time be at their disposal will be agencies and processes of destruction wholesale, unlimited, and perhaps, once launched, uncontrollable.

Mankind has never been in this position before. Without having improved appreciably in virtue or enjoying wiser guidance, it has got into its hands for the first time the tools by which it can unfailingly accomplish its own extermination. That is the point in

[3] From Winston S. Churchill, *Thoughts and Adventures* (London, 1932), pp. 248-50 and 252. Reprinted by permission of Odhams Press Limited, proprietors of the copyright. This essay was first published in pamphlet form as *Shall We Commit Suicide?* (New York, 1924).

human destinies to which all the glories and toils of men have at last led them. They would do well to pause and ponder upon their new responsibilities. Death stands at attention, obedient, expectant, ready to serve, ready to shear away the peoples en masse; ready, if called on, to pulverize, without hope of repair, what is left of civilization. He awaits only the word of command. He awaits it from a frail, bewildered being, long his victim, now—for one occasion only—his Master.

Let it not be thought for a moment that the danger of another explosion in Europe is passed. For the time being the stupor and the collapse which followed the World War ensure a sullen passivity, and the horror of war, its carnage and its tyrannies, has sunk into the soul, has dominated the mind, of every class in every race. But the causes of war have been in no way removed; indeed they are in some respects aggravated by the so-called Peace Treaties and the reactions following thereupon. Two mighty branches of the European family will never rest content with their existing situation. Russia, stripped of her Baltic Provinces, will, as the years pass by, brood incessantly upon the wars of Peter the Great. From one end of Germany to the other an intense hatred of France unites the whole population. The enormous contingents of German youth growing to military manhood year by year are inspired by the fiercest sentiments, and the soul of Germany smoulders with dreams of a War of Liberation or Revenge. These ideas are restrained at the present moment only by physical impotence. France is armed to the teeth. Germany has been to a great extent disarmed and her military system broken up. The French hope to preserve this situation by their technical military apparatus, by their shield of fortresses, by their black troops, and by a system of alliances with the smaller States of Europe; and for the present at any rate overwhelming force is on their side. But physical force alone, unsustained by world opinion, affords no durable foundation for security. Germany is a far stronger entity than France, and cannot be kept in permanent subjugation.

'Wars,' said a distinguished American to me some years ago, 'are fought with Steel; weapons may change, but Steel remains the core of all modern warfare. France has got the Steel of Europe, and Germany has lost it. Here, at any rate, is an element of permanency.' 'Are you sure,' I asked, 'that the wars of the future will be fought with Steel?' A few weeks later I talked with a German. 'What about

Aluminium?' he replied. 'Some think,' he said, 'that the next war will be fought with Electricity.' And on this a vista opens out of electrical rays which could paralyse the engines of a motor-car, could claw down aeroplanes from the sky, and conceivably be made destructive of human life or human vision. Then there are Explosives. Have we reached the end? Has Science turned its last page on them? May there not be methods of using explosive energy incomparably more intense than anything heretofore discovered? Might not a bomb no bigger than an orange be found to possess a secret power to destroy a whole block of buildings—nay, to concentrate the force of a thousand tons of cordite and blast a township at a stroke? Could not explosives even of the existing type be guided automatically in flying machines by wireless or other rays, without a human pilot, in ceaseless procession upon a hostile city, arsenal, camp, or dockyard?

Against the gathering but still distant tempest the League of Nations, deserted by the United States, scorned by Soviet Russia, flouted by Italy, distrusted equally by France and Germany, raises feebly but faithfully its standards of sanity and hope. Its structure, airy and unsubstantial, framed of shining but too often visionary idealism, is in its present form incapable of guarding the world from its dangers and of protecting mankind from itself. Yet it is through the League of Nations alone that the path to safety and salvation can be found. To sustain and aid the League of Nations is the duty of all. To reinforce it and bring it into vital and practical relation with actual world-politics by sincere agreements and understanding between the great Powers, between the leading races, should be the first aim of all who wish to spare their children torments and disasters compared with which those we have suffered will be but a pale preliminary.

It was to the League of Nations that Churchill continued to look for Europe's salvation. Ten years later he said:

I have been for the last few years trying to seek out for myself what would be the best way of preventing war, and it has seemed to me that the League of Nations should be the great instrument upon which all those resolved to maintain peace should centre, and that we should all make our contribution to the League of Nations. I should have thought that if there be Powers alarmed at the behaviour of their neighbours, they should refer to the League, and lay their anxieties before that body. It has seemed to me perfectly legitimate that the League of Nations should encourage the sanction of international authority for the formation of regional pacts between nations who may fear danger, and who seek to join hands together for mutual security against aggression. Therefore, I had the hope, I am bound to say, that the Government would not hesitate to further such developments. I cannot see how better you can prevent war than to confront an aggressor with the prospect of such a vast concentration of force, moral and material, that even the most reckless, even the most infuriated leader would not attempt to challenge those great forces. It seemed to me that if a number of agreements all under the sanction and authority of the League of Nations grew up between Powers who have anxieties, those Powers would naturally maintain forces which were adequate to enable them to discharge their duties and their obligations, and not try to weaken each other at all, because there is no greater danger than an approximation of force. If you wish to bring about war, you bring about such a balance that both sides think they have a chance of winning. If you want to stop war you gather such an aggregation of force on one side that the aggressor, whoever he may be, will not dare to challenge.

This process of agreements under the sanction of the League of Nations would eventually lead, I think, to a state which we should never exclude, namely, the ultimate creation of some international force, probably particularly in aviation, which would tend to place the security of nations upon a much higher foundation than it stands at present, and it seems to me you will never get such a development by arguing about matters purely in general. If there were, over a prolonged period of time, some general cause of anxiety, which all nations, or many nations, felt, then possibly forces might come together *ad hoc* for that purpose which, after that danger had happily been tided over, might still subsist permanently in amity.[4]

---

[4] From *Hansard,* July 13, 1934. Reprinted by permission of the Controller of Her Majesty's Stationery Office. See also Churchill's articles on the League reprinted in *Step By Step* (London, 1939).

ARMS FOR PEACE [5]

The British public were suspicious of Churchill's views on world affairs. They thought that he wished to pick a quarrel with the German and Italian dictatorships. But his only objective was security, without which he knew peace would be broken by any power which felt strong enough to do so. He spoke frequently in Parliament on the twin needs of armaments for national defense and of international cooperation for international security. He championed the rights of parliamentary democracy and of the League of Nations. But he now held no office in the Government. These were his wilderness years. Only a handful of his fellow countrymen listened carefully to what he was saying, or believed that peace was his real objective. After the Munich Agreement was signed by Hitler and Chamberlain, and the democratic Czechoslovakia dismembered to suit the dictator's demands, Churchill made one of his finest speeches, and at last succeeded in stirring the conscience of the British nation.

I find unendurable the sense of our country falling into the power, into the orbit and influence of Nazi Germany, and of our existence becoming dependent upon their goodwill or pleasure. It is to prevent that that I have tried my best to urge the maintenance of every bulwark of defense—first, the timely creation of an Air Force, superior to anything within striking distance of our shores; secondly, the gathering together of the collective strength of many nations; and thirdly, the making of alliances and military conventions, all within the covenant, in order to gather together forces at any rate to restrain the onward movement of this power. It has all been in vain. Every position had been successively undermined and abandoned on specious and plausible excuses. . . .

I do not grudge our loyal, brave people, who were ready to do their duty no matter what the cost, who never flinched under the strain of last week, I do not grudge them the natural, spontaneous

[5] From *Hansard*, October 5, 1938. Reprinted by permission of the Controller of Her Majesty's Stationery Office. This speech should be read in full. For Churchill's leading part in arguing against the appeasement policy of the British Government in the 1930s, see Martin Gilbert, *Britain and Germany Between the Wars* (London, 1964).

outburst of joy and relief when they learned that the hard ordeal would no longer be required of them, at the moment; but they should know the truth. They should know that there has been gross neglect and deficiency in our defenses; they should know that we have sustained a defeat without a war, the consequences of which will travel far with us along our road; they should know that we have passed an awful milestone in our history, when the whole equilibrium of Europe has been deranged, and that the terrible words have for the time being been pronounced against the Western democracies: "Thou art weighed in the balance and found wanting." And do not suppose that this is the end. This is only the beginning of the reckoning. This is only the first sip, the first foretaste of a bitter cup which will be proffered to us year by year unless, by a supreme recovery of moral health and martial vigor, we rise again and take our stand for freedom as in the olden time.

"AN IRON CURTAIN HAS DESCENDED"

After World War II Churchill again hoped to see the victors and vanquished united in a common purpose—the prevention of a third world holocaust. But one of the allies, the Soviet Union, under Stalin's leadership, pursued a policy which Churchill feared: the military domination of the small states of Eastern Europe and the drastic restriction of all political liberty. Churchill proposed two solutions: an alert but always defensive Anglo-American alliance, and a united Western Europe. The following two extracts show how he developed these ideas. The first is from his famous "Fulton" speech delivered in March 1946 at Westminster College, Fulton, Missouri; the second is from his speech at the first meeting of the Congress of Europe at the Hague in May 1948.

During his speech at Fulton Churchill said:

A shadow has fallen upon the scenes so lately lighted by the Allied victory. Nobody knows what Soviet Russia and its Communist international organisation intends to do in the immediate future, or what are the limits, if any, to its expansive and proselytising tendencies. I have a strong admiration and regard for the valiant Russian people and for my war-time comrade, Marshal Stalin. There is

deep sympathy and good will in Britain—and I doubt not here
also—towards the peoples of all the Russias, and a resolve to persevere through many differences and rebuffs in establishing lasting
friendships. We understand the Russian need to be secure on her
western frontiers by the removal of all possibility of German aggression. We welcome Russia to her rightful place among the leading
nations of the world. We welcome her flag upon the seas. Above all,
we welcome constant, frequent and growing contacts between the
Russian people and our own people on both sides of the Atlantic.
It is my duty, however, for I am sure you would wish me to state the
facts as I see them to you, to place before you certain facts about
the present position in Europe.

From Stettin in the Baltic to Trieste in the Adriatic, an iron
curtain has descended across the Continent. Behind that line lie
all the capitals of the ancient states of Central and Eastern Europe.
Warsaw, Berlin, Prague, Vienna, Budapest, Belgrade, Bucharest
and Sofia, all these famous cities and the populations around them
lie in what I must call the Soviet sphere, and all are subject in one
form or another, not only to Soviet influence but to a very high
and, in many cases, increasing measure of control from Moscow.
Athens alone—Greece with its immortal glories—is free to decide
its future at an election under British, American and French observation. The Russian-dominated Polish Government has been
encouraged to make enormous and wrongful inroads upon Germany, and mass expulsions of millions of Germans on a scale grievous and undreamed-of are now taking place. The Communist
parties, which were very small in all these Eastern States of Europe,
have been raised to pre-eminence and power far beyond their numbers and are seeking everywhere to obtain totalitarian control. Police
governments are prevailing in nearly every case, and so far, except
in Czechoslovakia, there is no true democracy.

Turkey and Persia are both profoundly alarmed and disturbed
at the claims which are being made upon them and at the pressure
being exerted by the Moscow Government. An attempt is being
made by the Russians in Berlin to build up a quasi-Communist
party in their zone of Occupied Germany by showing special favours
to groups of left-wing German leaders. At the end of the fighting
last June, the American and British armies withdrew westwards,
in accordance with an earlier Agreement, to a depth at some points

of one hundred and fifty miles upon a front of nearly four hundred miles, in order to allow our Russian allies to occupy this vast expanse of territory which the Western Democracies had conquered.

If now the Soviet Government tries, by separate action, to build up a pro-Communist Germany in their areas, this will cause new serious difficulties in the British and American zones, and will give the defeated Germans the power of putting themselves up to auction between the Soviets and the Western Democracies. Whatever conclusions may be drawn from these facts—and facts they are— this is certainly not the Liberated Europe we fought to build up. Nor is it one which contains the essentials of permanent peace.[6]

Churchill ended his speech at the Hague with a powerful plea:

President Roosevelt spoke of the Four Freedoms, but the one that matters most today is Freedom from Fear. Why should all these hardworking families be harassed, first in bygone times, by dynastic and religious quarrels, next by nationalistic ambitions, and finally by ideological fanaticism? Why should they now have to be regimented and hurled against each other by variously labelled forms of totalitarian tyranny, all fomented by wicked men, building their own predominance upon the misery and the subjugation of their fellow human beings? Why should so many millions of humble homes in Europe, aye, and much of its enlightenment and culture, sit quaking in dread of the policeman's knock? That is the question we have to answer here. After all, Europe has only to arise and stand in her own majesty, faithfulness and virtue, to confront all forms of tyranny, ancient or modern, Nazi or Communist, with forces which are unconquerable, and which if asserted in good time may never be challenged again.

I take a proud view of this Congress. We cannot rest upon benevolent platitudes and generalities. Our powers may be limited but we know and we must affirm what we mean and what we want. On the other hand it would not be wise in this critical time to be drawn into laboured attempts to rigid structures of constitutions. That is a later stage, and it is one in which the leadership must be

---

[6] Quoted in Winston S. Churchill, *The Second World War: Epilogue* (London, single volume edition, 1959), pp. 954-55, 956. Reprinted by permission of Houghton Mifflin Company.

taken by the ruling governments in response no doubt to our impulse, and in many cases to their own conceptions.

We are here to lay the foundations upon which the statesmen of the western democracies may stand, and to create an atmosphere favourable to the decisions to which they may be led. It is not for us who do not wield the authority of Governments to confront each other or the world with sharply-cut formulas or detailed arrangements. There are many different points of view which have to find their focus. We in Britain must move in harmony with our great partners in the Commonwealth, who, I do not doubt, though separated from us by the ocean spaces, share our aspirations and follow with deep attention our trend of thought. But undue precipitancy, like too much refinement, would hinder and not help the immediate mission we have to fulfil. Nevertheless we must not separate without a positive step forward. The task before us at this Congress is not only to raise the voice of United Europe during these few days we are together. We must here and now resolve that in one form or another a European Assembly shall be constituted which will enable that voice to make itself continuously heard and we trust with ever-growing acceptance through all the free countries of this Continent.

A high and a solemn responsibility rests upon us here this afternoon in this Congress of a Europe striving to be reborn. If we allow ourselves to be rent and disordered by pettiness and small disputes, if we fail in clarity of view or courage in action, a priceless occasion may be cast away for ever. But if we all pull together and pool the luck and the comradeship—and we shall need all the comradeship and not a little luck if we are to move together in this way—and firmly grasp the larger hopes of humanity, then it may be that we shall move into a happier sunlit age, when all the little children who are now growing up in this tormented world may find themselves not the victors nor the vanquished in the fleeting triumphs of one country over another in the bloody turmoil of destructive war, but the heirs of all the treasures of the past and the masters of all the science, the abundance and the glories of the future.[7]

[7] Quoted in Winston S. Churchill, *Europe Unite* (London, 1950), pp. 316-17. Reprinted by permission of Houghton Mifflin Company.

5
Defiance

In a long and varied life I have constantly watched and tried to measure the moods and inspirations of the British people. There is no foe they will not face. There is no hardship they cannot endure. Whether the test be short or long and wearisome, they can take it. What they do not forgive is false promises and vain boastings.

—CHURCHILL

Churchill was Britain's war leader for five years. During the first year of his Premiership Britain stood utterly alone after Hitler conquered Poland, Norway, Denmark, Holland, Belgium, and France. The Soviet Union and the United States stood aside. Militarily, Britain was isolated and vulnerable. It was at this desperate time that Churchill raised the spirit of the British people, rallied the downhearted, gave courage to those who were afraid, and persuaded the whole nation that it should resist Germany to the end, even if the end were bitter. This year of defiance, against heavy odds, was Churchill's finest hour.

"WE SHALL NEVER SURRENDER"[1]

In June 1940 the Germans drove the British Expeditionary Force back through France and Belgium to the sea. For a week they were in danger of total annihilation or capture. But 190,000 troops were rescued from the beaches by an armada of small ships under constant German bombardment. This was the "miracle of Dunkirk." It was also the end of British resistance in Europe, and seemed but the prelude to a German invasion of Britain itself. Churchill sought to rally the nation.

[1] From *Hansard*, June 4, 1940. Reprinted by permission of the Controller of Her Majesty's Stationery Office.

59

I have, myself, full confidence that if all do their duty, if nothing is neglected, and if the best arrangements are made, as they are being made, we shall prove ourselves once again able to defend our island home, to ride out the storm of war, and to outlive the menace of tyranny, if necessary for years, if necessary alone. At any rate, that is what we are going to try to do. That is the resolve of His Majesty's Government—every man of them. That is the will of Parliament and the nation. The British Empire and the French Republic, linked together in their cause and in their need, will defend to the death their native soil, aiding each other like good comrades to the utmost of their strength. Even though large tracts of Europe and many old and famous States have fallen or may fall into the grip of the Gestapo and all the odious apparatus of Nazi rule, we shall not flag or fail. We shall go on to the end, we shall fight in France, we shall fight on the seas and oceans, we shall fight with growing confidence and growing strength in the air, we shall defend our island, whatever the cost may be, we shall fight on the beaches, we shall fight on the landing grounds, we shall fight in the fields and in the streets, we shall fight in the hills; we shall never surrender, and even if, which I do not for a moment believe, this island or a large part of it were subjugated and starving, then our Empire beyond the seas, armed and guarded by the British Fleet, would carry on the struggle, until, in God's good time, the new world, with all its power and might, steps forth to the rescue and the liberation of the old.

THE FALL OF FRANCE [2]

On June 14, 1940, the Germans occupied Paris. Three days later a new French Government, led by Marshal Pétain, sued for peace. Churchill broadcast to the British people.

The news from France is very bad and I grieve for the gallant French people who have fallen into this terrible misfortune. Noth-

[2] From a speech also delivered in the House of Commons, on June 4, 1940. This and the following five speeches were first broadcast over the British Broadcasting Corporation network and were at once reprinted fully in most British and American newspapers. I have used the texts as printed in Winston S. Churchill, *Into Battle* (London, 1941), and *The Unrelenting Struggle* (London, 1942), with permission of Houghton Mifflin Company.

ing will alter our feelings towards them or our faith that the genius of France will rise again. What has happened in France makes no difference to our actions and purpose. We have become the sole champions now in arms to defend the world cause. We shall do our best to be worthy of this high honour. We shall defend our island home and with the British Empire we shall fight on unconquerable until the curse of Hitler is lifted from the brows of mankind. We are sure that in the end all will come right.

AWAITING THE GERMAN INVASION [3]

In September 1940 the Germans began their heaviest bombing raids of the war, on London. No one knew when the invasion would be launched. Almost everyone assumed that it would be within a matter of days. Churchill broadcast courage and defiance to the people, many of whom now thought that the best policy might be to make a compromise peace with Germany.

We cannot tell when they will try to come; we cannot be sure that in fact they will try at all; but no one should blind himself to the fact that a heavy, full-scale invasion of this island is being prepared with all the usual German thoroughness and method, and that it may be launched now—upon England, upon Scotland, or upon Ireland, or upon all three.

If this invasion is going to be tried at all, it does not seem that it can be long delayed. The weather may break at any time. Besides this, it is difficult for the enemy to keep these gatherings of ships waiting about indefinitely, while they are bombed every night by our bombers, and very often shelled by our warships which are waiting for them outside.

Therefore, we must regard the next week or so as a very important period in our history. It ranks with the days when the Spanish Armada was approaching the Channel, and Drake was finishing his game of bowls; or when Nelson stood between us and Napoleon's Grand Army at Boulogne. We have read all about this in the history books; but what is happening now is on a far greater scale and of far

[3] Quoted in Winston S. Churchill, *Into Battle* (London, 1941), p. 224. Reprinted by permission of Houghton Mifflin Company.

more consequence to the life and future of the world and its civilisation than these brave old days of the past.

Every man and woman will therefore prepare himself to do his duty, whatever it may be, with special pride and care. Our fleets and flotillas are very powerful and numerous; our Air Force is at the highest strength it has ever reached, and it is conscious of its proved superiority, not indeed in numbers, but in men and machines. Our shores are well fortified and strongly manned, and behind them, ready to attack the invaders, we have a far larger and better equipped mobile Army than we have ever had before.

Besides this, we have more than a million and a half men of the Home Guard, who are just as much soldiers of the Regular Army as the Grenadier Guards, and who are determined to fight for every inch of the ground in every village and in every street.

It is with devout but sure confidence that I say: Let God defend the Right.

These cruel, wanton, indiscriminate bombings of London are, of course, a part of Hitler's invasion plans. He hopes, by killing large numbers of civilians, and women and children, that he will terrorise and cow the people of this mighty imperial city, and make them a burden and an anxiety to the Government and thus distract our attention unduly from the ferocious onslaught he is preparing. Little does he know the spirit of the British nation, or the tough fibre of the Londoners, whose forbears played a leading part in the establishment of Parliamentary institutions and who have been bred to value freedom far above their lives. This wicked man, the repository and embodiment of many forms of soul-destroying hatred, this monstrous product of former wrongs and shame, has now resolved to try to break our famous island race by a process of indiscriminate slaughter and destruction. What he has done is to kindle a fire in British hearts, here and all over the world, which will glow long after all traces of the conflagration he has caused in London have been removed. He has lighted a fire which will burn with a steady and consuming flame until the last vestiges of Nazi tyranny have been burnt out of Europe, and until the Old World—and the New—can join hands to rebuild the temples of man's freedom and man's honour, upon foundations which will not soon or easily be overthrown.

"RE-ARM YOUR SPIRITS" [4]

*In October 1940 Churchill sought to encourage the French
people, who were then subjected to the full rigor of German
rule and Nazi control.*

Frenchmen! For more than thirty years in peace and war I
have marched with you, and I am marching still along the same
road. To-night I speak to you at your firesides wherever you may
be, or whatever your fortunes are. I repeat the prayer around the
louis d'or, "Dieu protège la France." Here at home in England,
under the fire of the Boche, we do not forget the ties and links that
unite us to France, and we are persevering steadfastly and in good
heart in the cause of European freedom and fair dealing for the
common people of all countries, for which, with you, we drew the
sword. When good people get into trouble because they are attacked
and heavily smitten by the vile and wicked, they must be very careful not to get at loggerheads with one another. The common
enemy is always trying to bring this about, and, of course, in bad
luck a lot of things happen which play into the enemy's hands. We
must just make the best of things as they come along.

Here in London, which Herr Hitler says he will reduce to ashes,
and which his aeroplanes are now bombarding, our people are bearing up unflinchingly. Our Air Force has more than held its own. We
are waiting for the long-promised invasion. So are the fishes. But, of
course, this for us is only the beginning. Now in 1940, in spite of
occasional losses, we have, as ever, command of the seas. In 1941 we
shall have the command of the air. Remember what that means.
Herr Hitler with his tanks and other mechanical weapons, and also
by Fifth Column intrigue with traitors, has managed to subjugate
for the time being most of the finest races in Europe, and his little
Italian accomplice is trotting along hopefully and hungrily, but
rather wearily and very timidly, at his side. They both wish to carve
up France and her Empire as if it were a fowl: to one a leg, to
another a wing or perhaps part of the breast. Not only the French

[4] From an address broadcast in French and English, October 21, 1940. Quoted
in Winston S. Churchill, *Into Battle* (London, 1941), pp. 295-97. Reprinted by
permission of Houghton Mifflin Company.

Empire will be devoured by these two ugly customers, but Alsace-Lorraine will go once again under the German yoke, and Nice, Savoy and Corsica—Napoleon's Corsica—will be torn from the fair realm of France. But Herr Hitler is not thinking only of stealing other people's territories, or flinging gobbets of them to his little confederate. I tell you truly what you must believe when I say this evil man, this monstrous abortion of hatred and defeat, is resolved on nothing less than the complete wiping out of the French nation, and the disintegration of its whole life and future. By all kinds of sly and savage means, he is plotting and working to quench for ever the fountain of characteristic French culture and of French inspiration to the world. All Europe, if he has his way, will be reduced to one uniform Boche-land, to be exploited, pillaged, and bullied by his Nazi gangsters. You will excuse my speaking frankly because this is not a time to mince words. It is not defeat that France will now be made to suffer at German hands, but the doom of complete obliteration. Army, Navy, Air Force, religion, law, language, culture, institutions, literature, history, tradition, all are to be effaced by the brute strength of a triumphant Army and the scientific low-cunning of a ruthless Police Force.

Frenchmen—re-arm your spirits before it is too late. Remember how Napoleon said before one of his battles: "These same Prussians who are so boastful to-day were three to one at Jena, and six to one at Montmirail." Never will I believe that the soul of France is dead. Never will I believe that her place amongst the greatest nations of the world has been lost for ever! All these schemes and crimes of Herr Hitler's are bringing upon him and upon all who belong to his system a retribution which many of us will live to see. The story is not yet finished, but it will not be so long. We are on his track, and so are our friends across the Atlantic Ocean, and your friends across the Atlantic Ocean. If he cannot destroy us, we will surely destroy him and all his gang, and all their works. Therefore, have hope and faith, for all will come right.

Now what is it we British ask of you in this present hard and bitter time? What we ask at this moment in our struggle to win the victory which we will share with you, is that if you cannot help us, at least you will not hinder us. Presently you will be able to weight the arm that strikes for you, and you ought to do so. But even now we believe that Frenchmen wherever they may be, feel their hearts warm and a proud blood tingle in their veins when we have some success in the air or on the sea, or presently—for that will come—upon the land.

Remember we shall never stop, never weary, and never give in, and that our whole people and Empire have vowed themselves to the task of cleansing Europe from the Nazi pestilence and saving the world from the new Dark Ages. Do not imagine, as the German-controlled wireless tells you, that we English seek to take your ships and colonies. We seek to beat the life and soul out of Hitler and Hitlerism. That alone, that all the time, that to the end. We do not covet anything from any nation except their respect. Those Frenchmen who are in the French Empire, and those who are in so-called unoccupied France, may see their way from time to time to useful action. I will not go into details. Hostile ears are listening. As for those, to whom English hearts go out in full, because they see them under the sharp discipline, oppression, and spying of the Hun—as to those Frenchmen in the occupied regions, to them I say, when they think of the future let them remember the words which Gambetta, that great Frenchman, uttered after 1870 about the future of France and what was to come: "Think of it always: speak of it never."

Good night then: sleep to gather strength for the morning. For the morning will come. Brightly will it shine on the brave and true, kindly upon all who suffer for the cause, glorious upon the tombs of heroes. Thus will shine the dawn. *Vive la France!* Long live also the forward march of the common people in all the lands towards their just and true inheritance, and towards the broader and fuller age.

"ALL WILL COME RIGHT" [5]

On June 12, 1941, in a speech to Dominion High Commissioners and Allied Ministers, Churchill, after over a year as Prime Minister, again rallied the British people and filled them with confidence in the outcome of the war. His optimism and defiance were the twin pillars of his power. No amount of guns, tanks, or planes could create the same faith in ultimate victory.

[5] From a speech broadcast on June 12, 1941. Quoted in Winston S. Churchill, *The Unrelenting Struggle* (London, 1942), pp. 171-72. Reprinted by permission of Houghton Mifflin Company.

We cannot yet see how deliverance will come, or when it will
come, but nothing is more certain than that every trace of Hitler's
footsteps, every stain of his infected and corroding fingers will be
sponged and purged and, if need be, blasted from the surface of
the earth.

We are here to affirm and fortify our union in that ceaseless and
unwearying effort which must be made if the captive peoples are to
be set free. A year ago His Majesty's Government was left alone
to face the storm, and to many of our friends and enemies alike it
may have seemed that our days too were numbered, and that Britain
and its institutions would sink for ever beneath the verge. But I
may with some pride remind your Excellencies that, even in that
dark hour when our Army was disorganized and almost weaponless,
when scarcely a gun or a tank remained in Britain, when almost
all our stores and ammunition had been lost in France, never for
one moment did the British people dream of making peace with the
conqueror, and never for a moment did they despair of the common
cause. On the contrary, we proclaimed at that very time to all men,
not only to ourselves, our determination not to make peace until
every one of the ravaged and enslaved countries was liberated and
until the Nazi domination was broken and destroyed.

See how far we have travelled since those breathless days of
June a year ago. Our solid, stubborn strength has stood the awful
test. We are masters of our own air, and now reach out in ever-
growing retribution upon the enemy. The Royal Navy holds the
seas. The Italian fleet cowers diminished in harbour, the German
Navy is largely crippled or sunk. The murderous raids upon our
ports, cities, and factories have been powerless to quench the spirit
of the British nation, to stop our national life, or check the immense expansion of our war industry. The food and arms from
across the oceans are coming safely in. Full provision to replace all
sunken tonnage is being made here, and still more by our friends
in the United States. We are becoming an armed community. Our
land forces are being perfected in equipment and training.

Hitler may turn and trample this way and that through tortured
Europe. He may spread his course far and wide, and carry his curse
with him: he may break into Africa or into Asia. But it is here, in
this island fortress, that he will have to reckon in the end. We
shall strive to resist by land and sea. We shall be on his track

wherever he goes. Our air power will continue to teach the German homeland that war is not all loot and triumph.

We shall aid and stir the people of every conquered country to resistance and revolt. We shall break up and derange every effort which Hitler makes to systematize and consolidate his subjugation. He will find no peace, no rest, no halting-place, no parley. And if, driven to desperate hazards, he attempts the invasion of the British Isles, as well he may, we shall not flinch from the supreme trial. With the help of God, of which we must all feel daily conscious, we shall continue steadfast in faith and duty till our task is done.

This, then, is the message which we send forth to-day to all the States and nations bond or free, to all the men in all the lands who care for freedom's cause, to our allies and well-wishers in Europe, to our American friends and helpers drawing ever closer in their might across the ocean: this is the message—Lift up your hearts. All will come right. Out of the depths of sorrow and sacrifice will be born again the glory of mankind.

A CALL TO AMERICA: "TIME IS SHORT" [6]

Only four days later, on June 16, Churchill made a stirring appeal to the United States, for whose direct military intervention in the war he had so far prayed in vain. In this broadcast to the United States he put before the American people the full meaning of Britain's struggle.

I am grateful, President Valentine, for the honour which you have conferred upon me in making me a Doctor of Laws of Rochester University in the State of New York. I am extremely complimented by the expressions of praise and commendation in which you have addressed me, not because I am or ever can be worthy of them, but because they are an expression of American confidence and affection which I shall ever strive to deserve.

But what touches me most in this ceremony is that sense of kinship and of unity which I feel exists between us this afternoon. As I speak from Downing Street to Rochester University and through you to the people of the United States, I almost feel I have the right to do

[6] Quoted in Winston S. Churchill, *The Unrelenting Struggle* (London, 1942), pp. 173-75. Reprinted by permission of Houghton Mifflin Company.

so, because my mother, as you have stated, was born in your city, and here my grandfather, Leonard Jerome, lived for so many years, conducting as a prominent and rising citizen a newspaper with the excellent eighteenth-century title of the *Plain Dealer*.

The great Burke has truly said, "People will not look forward to posterity who never look backward to their ancestors," and I feel it most agreeable to recall to you that the Jeromes were rooted for many generations in American soil, and fought in Washington's Armies for the independence of the American Colonies and the foundation of the United States. I expect I was on both sides then. And I must say I feel on both sides of the Atlantic Ocean now.

At intervals during the last forty years I have addressed scores of great American audiences in almost every part of the Union. I have learnt to admire the courtesy of these audiences; their sense of fair play; their sovereign sense of humour, never minding the joke that is turned against themselves; their earnest, voracious desire to come to the root of the matter and to be well and truly informed on Old World affairs.

And now, in this time of world storm, when I have been called upon by King and Parliament and with the support of all parties in the State to bear the chief responsibility in Great Britain, and when I have had the supreme honour of speaking for the British nation in its most deadly danger and in its finest hour, it has given me comfort and inspiration to feel that I think as you do, that our hands are joined across the oceans, and that our pulses throb and beat as one. Indeed I will make so bold as to say that here at least, in my mother's birth city of Rochester, I hold a latchkey to American hearts.

Strong tides of emotion, fierce surges of passion, sweep the broad expanses of the Union in this year of fate. In that prodigious travail there are many elemental forces, there is much heart-searching and self-questioning; some pangs, some sorrow, some conflict of voices, but no fear. The world is witnessing the birth throes of a sublime resolve. I shall presume to confess to you that I have no doubts what that resolve will be.

The destiny of mankind is not decided by material computation. When great causes are on the move in the world, stirring all men's souls, drawing them from their firesides, casting aside comfort, wealth, and the pursuit of happiness in response to impulses at once awe-striking and irresistible, we learn that we are spirits, not animals, and that something is going on in space and time, and beyond space and time, which, whether we like it or not, spells duty.

A wonderful story is unfolding before our eyes. How it will end we are not allowed to know. But on both sides of the Atlantic we all feel, I repeat, all, that we are a part of it, that our future and that of many generations is at stake. We are sure that the character of human society will be shaped by the resolves we take and the deeds we do. We need not bewail the fact that we have been called upon to face such solemn responsibilities. We may be proud, and even rejoice amid our tribulations, that we have been born at this cardinal time for so great an age and so splendid an opportunity of service here below.

Wickedness, enormous, panoplied, embattled, seemingly triumphant, casts its shadow over Europe and Asia. Laws, customs, and traditions are broken up. Justice is cast from her seat. The rights of the weak are trampled down. The grand freedoms of which the President of the United States has spoken so movingly are spurned and chained. The whole stature of man, his genius, his initiative, and his nobility, is ground down under systems of mechanical barbarism and of organized and scheduled terror.

For more than a year we British have stood alone, uplifted by your sympathy and respect and sustained by our own unconquerable will-power and by the increasing growth and hopes of your massive aid. In these British islands that look so small upon the map we stand, the faithful guardians of the rights and dearest hopes of a dozen States and nations now gripped and tormented in a base and cruel servitude. Whatever happens we shall endure to the end.

But what is the explanation of the enslavement of Europe by the German Nazi régime? How did they do it? It is but a few years ago since one united gesture by the peoples, great and small, who are now broken in the dust, would have warded off from mankind the fearful ordeal it has had to undergo. But there was no unity. There was no vision. The nations were pulled down one by one while the others gaped and chattered. One by one, each in his turn, they let themselves be caught. One after another they were felled by brutal violence or poisoned from within by subtle intrigue.

And now the old lion with her lion cubs at her side stands alone against hunters who are armed with deadly weapons and impelled by desperate and destructive rage. Is the tragedy to repeat itself once more? Ah no! This is not the end of the tale. The stars in their courses proclaim the deliverance of mankind. Not so easily shall the onward progress of the peoples be barred. Not so easily shall the lights of freedom die.

But time is short. Every month that passes adds to the length and to the perils of the journey that will have to be made. United we stand. Divided we fall. Divided, the dark age returns. United, we can save and guide the world.

ALLIANCE WITH RUSSIA: "THIS IS NO CLASS WAR" [7]

Within a week, on June 22, 1941, Hitler invaded the Soviet Union. The world waited anxiously to hear Britain's reaction. Would she stand aside and watch Nazism and Communism seek to destroy each other? Would she hope to see Hitler exhaust himself in the vast expanse of Russia? Churchill decided, without any hesitation, on a bold and unexpected step. He announced that Britain would consider herself forthwith Russia's ally, and would cooperate fully with Russia until Nazism was destroyed. At last Britain had a partner in the fight against tyranny. And Churchill's broadcast which welcomed that partner to Britain's side electrified occupied Europe. Those millions who lived under Nazi dominion and terror, and who heard his words illegally on secret radios, or passed news of them in whispers at street corners, realized in an instant that Britain was fighting not merely for national survival, but for the cause of free men everywhere. Churchill's strong hostility to Communism after the 1917 Revolution was well known; it made his declaration of Anglo-Soviet unity even more impressive.

No one has been a more consistent opponent of Communism than I have for the last twenty-five years. I will unsay no word that I have spoken about it. But all this fades away before the spectacle which is now unfolding. The past with its crimes, its follies and its tragedies, flashes away. I see the Russian soldiers standing on the threshold of their native land, guarding the fields which their fathers

[7] Quoted in Winston S. Churchill, *The Unrelenting Struggle* (London, 1942), pp. 178-80. Reprinted by permission of Houghton Mifflin Company.

have tilled from time immemorial. I see them guarding their homes where mothers and wives pray—ah yes, for there are times when all pray—for the safety of their loved ones, the return of the bread-winner, of their champion, of their protector. I see the ten thousand villages of Russia, where the means of existence was wrung so hardly from the soil, but where there are still primordial human joys, where maidens laugh and children play. I see advancing upon all this in hideous onslaught the Nazi war machine, with its clanking, heel-clicking, dandified Prussian officers, its crafty expert agents fresh from the cowing and tying-down of a dozen countries. I see also the dull, drilled, docile, brutish masses of the Hun soldiery plodding on like a swarm of crawling locusts. I see the German bombers and fighters in the sky, still smarting from many a British whipping, delighted to find what they believe is an easier and a safer prey.

Behind all this glare, behind all this storm, I see that small group of villainous men who plan, organize and launch this cataract of horrors upon mankind. And then my mind goes back across the years to the days when the Russian armies were our allies against the same deadly foe; when they fought with so much valour and constancy, and helped to gain a victory from all share in which, alas, they were —through no fault of ours—utterly cut off. I have lived through all this, and you will pardon me if I express my feelings and the stir of old memories.

But now I have to declare the decision of His Majesty's Government—and I feel sure it is a decision in which the great Dominions will, in due course, concur—for we must speak out now, at once, without a day's delay. I have to make the declaration, but can you doubt what our policy will be? We have but one aim and one single, irrevocable purpose. We are resolved to destroy Hitler and every vestige of the Nazi régime. From this nothing will turn us—nothing. We will never parley, we will never negotiate with Hitler or any of his gang. We shall fight him by land, we shall fight him by sea, we shall fight him in the air, until with God's help we have rid the earth of his shadow and liberated its peoples from his yoke. Any man or state who fights on against Nazidom will have our aid. Any man or state who marches with Hitler is our foe. . . . That is our policy and that is our declaration. It follows, therefore, that we shall give whatever help we can to Russia and the Russian people. We shall appeal to all our friends and allies in every part of the world to take the same course and pursue it, as we shall, faithfully and steadfastly to the end.

We have offered the Government of Soviet Russia any technical or economic assistance which is in our power, and which is likely to be of service to them. We shall bomb Germany by day as well as by night in ever-increasing measure, casting upon them month by month a heavier discharge of bombs, and making the German people taste and gulp each month a sharper dose of the miseries they have showered upon mankind. It is noteworthy that only yesterday the Royal Air Force, fighting inland over French territory, cut down with very small loss to themselves 28 of the Hun fighting machines in the air above the French soil they have invaded, defiled and profess to hold. But this is only a beginning. From now forward the main expansion of our Air Force proceeds with gathering speed. In another six months the weight of the help we are receiving from the United States in war materials of all kinds, and especially in heavy bombers, will begin to tell.

This is no class war, but a war in which the whole British Empire and Commonwealth of Nations is engaged without distinction of race, creed or party. It is not for me to speak of the action of the United States, but this I will say: if Hitler imagines that his attack on Soviet Russia will cause the slightest division of aims or slackening of effort in the great Democracies who are resolved upon his doom, he is woefully mistaken. On the contrary, we shall be fortified and encouraged in our efforts to rescue mankind from his tyranny. We shall be strengthened and not weakened in determination and in resources.

This is no time to moralize on the follies of countries and governments which have allowed themselves to be struck down one by one, when by united action they could have saved themselves and saved the world from this catastrophe. But when I spoke a few minutes ago of Hitler's blood-lust and the hateful appetites which have impelled or lured him on his Russian adventure, I said there was one deeper motive behind his outrage. He wishes to destroy the Russian power because he hopes that if he succeeds in this, he will be able to bring back the main strength of his army and air force from the East and hurl it upon this Island, which he knows he must conquer or suffer the penalty of his crimes. His invasion of Russia is no more than a prelude to an attempted invasion of the British Isles. He hopes, no doubt, that all this may be accomplished before the winter comes, and that he can overwhelm Great Britain before the fleet and air power of the United States may intervene. He hopes that he may once again repeat, upon a greater scale than ever before, that process of destroying his enemies one by one, by which he has so long thrived and prospered, and that then the scene will be clear for the final act, without which all his conquests would be in vain—namely, the subjugation of the Western Hemisphere to his will and to his system.

The Russian danger is therefore our danger, and the danger of the United States, just as the cause of any Russian fighting for his hearth and home is the cause of free men and free peoples in every quarter of the globe. Let us learn the lessons already taught by such cruel experience. Let us redouble our exertions, and strike with united strength while life and power remain.

THE GRAND ALLIANCE: "THE SLEEP OF THE SAVED" [8]

Churchill was disappointed in his hope that the United States would declare war on Hitler. But when the Japanese bombed Pearl Harbor on December 7, 1941, Hitler himself declared war on the United States. This action brought the United States to Britain's side. Thus, by the stupidity of Britain's enemies, the limitless and ultimately decisive power of the New World was joined to that of the Old. Of this black day in American history Churchill wrote:

No American will think it wrong of me if I proclaim that to have the United States at our side was to me the greatest joy. I could not foretell the course of events. I do not pretend to have measured accurately the martial might of Japan, but now at this very moment I knew the United States was in the war, up to the neck and in to the death. So we had won after all! Yes, after Dunkirk; after the fall of France; after the horrible episode of Oran; after the threat of invasion, when, apart from the Air and the Navy, we

[8] From Winston S. Churchill, *The Second World War,* Vol. III, *The Grand Alliance* (London, 1950), pp. 539-40. Quoted by permission of Houghton Mifflin Company.

were an almost unarmed people; after the deadly struggle of the U-boat war—the first Battle of the Atlantic, gained by a hand's-breadth; after seventeen months of lonely fighting and nineteen months of my responsibility in dire stress. We had won the war. England would live; Britain would live; the Commonwealth of Nations and the Empire would live. How long the war would last or in what fashion it would end no man could tell, nor did I at this moment care. Once again in our long Island history we should emerge, however mauled or mutilated, safe and victorious. We should not be wiped out. Our history would not come to an end. We might not even have to die as individuals. Hitler's fate was sealed. Mussolini's fate was sealed. As for the Japanese, they would be ground to powder. All the rest was merely the proper application of overwhelming force. The British Empire, the Soviet Union, and now the United States, bound together with every scrap of their life and strength, were, according to my lights, twice or even thrice the force of their antagonists. No doubt it would take a long time. I expected terrible forfeits in the East; but all this would be merely a passing phase. United we could subdue everybody else in the world. Many disasters, immeasurable cost and tribulation lay ahead, but there was no more doubt about the end.

Silly people, and there were many, not only in enemy countries, might discount the force of the United States. Some said they were soft, others that they would never be united. They would fool around at a distance. They would never come to grips. They would never stand bloodletting. Their democracy and system of recurrent elections would paralyse their war effort. They would be just a vague blur on the horizon to friend or foe. Now we should see the weakness of this numerous but remote, wealthy, and talkative people. But I had studied the American Civil War, fought out to the last desperate inch. American blood flowed in my veins. I thought of a remark which Edward Grey had made to me more than thirty years before—that the United States is like a "gigantic boiler. Once the fire is lighted under it there is no limit to the power it can generate." Being saturated and satiated with emotion and sensation, I went to bed and slept the sleep of the saved and thankful.

PART TWO

THE WORLD LOOKS AT CHURCHILL

*The truth is incontrovertible. Panic may resent it;
ignorance may deride it; malice may distort it, but
there it is.*

—CHURCHILL

*Throughout his life Churchill was a source of public
controversy and comment. There is hardly a volume of memoirs written after the turn of the century in which he does not
figure. As he was constantly active in a wide range of political
matters, was a lively and provocative speaker, and tended to
comment publicly on anything about which he felt strongly,
it is not surprising that so much was written about him during
his lifetime. Many people, not all of them politicians, sought
at different times to write down their impressions of him and
to analyze his character as they saw it. In the following extracts
I have chosen what I hope is a representative selection of the
different feelings which he aroused.*

G. W. STEEVENS: BORN TO LEAD [1]

*In 1898 G. W. Steevens, a newspaper correspondent during
the reconquest of the Sudan, traveled back to England from
the war with Lieutenant Churchill. In his account, which was
published that same year in the London* Daily Mail, *he
proved a shrewd and prophetic observer. Churchill was not
then twenty-four years old.*

Winston Spencer Churchill is the youngest man in Europe. A
gallery of young men's pictures could not possibly be complete without him, for there is no younger.

[1] First published on December 2, 1898, in the *Daily Mail*. Reprinted by permission of Associated Newspapers Ltd. Steevens, who became a close friend of
Churchill's, died of typhoid fever during the Boer War. Churchill wrote of him
that "his gay, mocking spirit and rippling wit made him a delightful companion"
(*My Early Life*, p. 228).

In years he is a boy; in temperament he is also a boy; but in intention, in deliberate plan, purpose, adaptation of means to ends he is already a man. In any other generation but this he would be a child. Anyone other than him, being a junior subaltern of Hussars, would be a boisterous, simple, full-hearted, empty-headed boy. But Churchill is a man, with ambitions fixed, with the steps towards their attainment clearly defined, with a precocious, almost uncanny judgment as to the efficacy of the means to the end.

He is what he is by breeding. He is the eldest son of Lord Randolph Churchill, and his mother is American. Lord Randolph was not so precocious as he was popularly supposed to be, but they begin early in America. From his father he derives the hereditary aptitude for affairs, the grand style of entering upon them, which are not the less hereditary in British noble families because they skip nine generations out of ten. Winston Spencer Churchill can hardly have seen much of Government and Parliament and forensic politics at twenty-four, but he moves in and out among their deviations with the ease, if not with the knowledge, of a veteran statesman. But that inheritance alone would not give him his grip and facility at twenty-four; with us hereditary statesmen and party leaders ripen later. From his American strain he adds to this a keenness, a shrewdness, a half-cynical, personal ambition, a natural aptitude for advertisement, and, happily, a sense of humour.

At the present moment he happens to be a soldier, but that has nothing whatever to do with his interest in the public eye. He may and he may not possess the qualities which make a great general, but the question is of no sort of importance. In any case, they will never be developed, for, if they exist, they are overshadowed by qualities which might make him, almost at will, a great popular leader, a great journalist, or the founder of a great advertising business.

He will shortly leave the Army; in the meantime his brief military career is interesting, mainly as an illustration of the versatility, the pushing energy, and—its complement—the precocious worldly wisdom of the man. Educated at Harrow, he passed, like anybody else, into Sandhurst, at eighteen, in 1893, passed out with honours in 1894, joined the 4th Hussars in 1895. From that till now is less than four years; yet in that time he has seen something of three campaigns —not an ungenerous allowance for a field-officer of more service than Winston Spencer Churchill counts years of life. He saw his service, it is true, more in the irresponsible way of war correspondent than on the plodding grind of a subaltern with his regiment; but then that is the only way—bar miracles—in which a man can see three campaigns in four years. Having to give the first years of his manhood to war-making, he characteristically gave them in the way that was likely to prove most fruitful of experience for use afterwards.

Before he had been a year in the Army he was in Cuba, travelled over much of the island, saw a certain amount of service, got the Order of Military Merit from Marshal Martinez Campos, and wrote letters to the Daily Graphic. In the last frontier war in India he started as the correspondent of the Daily Telegraph and The Pioneer—to what other subaltern of twenty-two would it have occurred to syndicate himself thus fruitfully?—went on to the 31st Punjab Infantry, was mentioned for "courage and resolution" by Brigadier-General Jeffreys, and wound up as orderly officer to Sir William Lockhart. What other subaltern of twenty-two would have gone through so many phases? To top all he was author of the first book published on the series of campaigns—The Story of the Malakand Field Force—and the book was a decided success.

How many men had the combination of merit, energy, and luck to combine the Tirah clasps with Khartoum? Very few, but among the few duly appeared Winston Churchill. He got up just in time to march from Fort Atbara with the 21st Lancers, to which he was attached—missed them, indeed by a day, but rode out confidently at night, missed the track, lit matches and found it, had to turn miles out of his way for water, overtook the force next day. He finished the march, scouted in the reconnaissances, rode in the charge. Now —you will have guessed—he is writing a book. And yet he found time on his way home to prepare three political speeches.

It was not possible that a man who has done so much so well at twenty-four would be altogether popular. Enemies he had probably none, but precocious success is not the way to win facile friendship —even when joined with modesty—and Winston Churchill is, outwardly, not modest. In the Army especially, where the young are expected not to know better than their elders—or, at least, to keep their knowledge to themselves—his assurance has earned him many snubs. One general will delight in his light-hearted omniscience, the next, and the next, and the next will put a subaltern in his place. But Winston Churchill cannot be snubbed. His self-confidence bobs up irresistibly, though seniority and common sense and facts themselves conspire to force it down.

After all he is hardly to be charged with any but outward immodesty. Chaff him about his self-satisfaction and he laughs and says, "I'm young." He knows he is not omniscient; but he knows it will pay to pretend to be.

He is ambitious and he is calculating; yet he is not cold—and that saves him. His ambition is sanguine, runs in a torrent, and the calculation is hardly more than the rocks or the stump which the torrent strikes for a second, yet which suffices to direct its course. It is not so much that he calculates how he is to make his career a success—how, frankly, he is to boom—but that he has a queer, shrewd power of introspection, which tells him his gifts and character are such as will make him boom. He has not studied to make himself a demagogue. He was born a demagogue, and he happens to know it.

The master strain in his character is the rhetorician. Platform speeches and leading articles flow from him almost against his will. At dinner he talks and talks, and you can hardly tell when he leaves off quoting his one idol, Macaulay, and begins his other, Winston Churchill. A passionate devotion to the matter in hand, an imperturbable self-confidence, a ready flow of sonorous, half-commonplace, half-lofty English, a fine faculty of striking imagery—we shall hear more about this in the course of ten years. Out of the perfect stump orator's wallet he has taken everything but humour; his humour he is likely to keep for private moments; he is not yet the man who, like Lord Rosebery, will feel he can afford to smile at himself in public.

His face is square and determined rather than delicate, his body fitter for the platform than for the saddle; his colour reddish and sanguine. He looks a boy. As yet, naturally, he knows little more than many clever boys, whether of faces or of men. But for all that he has put himself in the directest way of learning. At present he calls himself a Tory Democrat. Tory—the opinions—might change; democrat—the methods—never. For he has the twentieth century in his marrow.

What he will become, who shall say? At the rate he goes there will hardly be room for him in Parliament at thirty or in England at forty. It is a pace that cannot last, yet already he holds a vast lead of his contemporaries. Meanwhile he is a wonder—a boy with a man's ambitions and—more wonderful yet—a very mature man's self-appreciation—knowledge of his own powers and the extent to which each may be applied to set him forward on his road.

CONSUELO VANDERBILT: "THE DEMOCRATIC SPIRIT" [2]

Consuelo Vanderbilt, the American heiress, was married to Churchill's cousin, the Duke of Marlborough. Her account of her first meeting with him in 1900, when he was campaigning for Parliament, is a vivid one.

I remember my first experience of a British election with him at Oldham in Lancashire. Listening to his speeches or driving with him in an open carriage through cheering crowds was equally exciting, for already he possessed the flame that kindles enthusiasm. I noted his frequent references to his father, Lord Randolph Churchill, and was struck by his evident admiration and respectful reverence for him; I had a presentiment that inspired with such memories he would seek to emulate him!

Winston was then the life and soul of the young and brilliant circle that gathered round him at Blenheim: a circle in which the women matched their beauty against the more intellectual attractions of the men. Whether it is his American blood or his boyish enthusiasm and spontaneity, qualities sadly lacking in my husband, I delighted in his companionship. His conversation was invariably stimulating, and his views on life were not drawn and quartered, as were Marlborough's, by a sense of self-importance. To me he represented the democratic spirit so foreign to my environment, and which I deeply missed.

ST. JOHN BRODRICK: REBUKE FOR THE RENEGADE [3]

Churchill's parliamentary colleagues observed him in a hostile light when, as a very junior Conservative Member of

[2] From Consuelo Vanderbilt Balsan, *The Glitter and The Gold* (London, 1953), p. 103. Reprinted by permission of Harper & Row, Publishers, Inc.

[3] From *Hansard*, May 16, 1901. Reprinted by permission of the Controller of Her Majesty's Stationery Office.

Parliament, he attacked the military expenditure of his own Conservative Ministers. In this selection the Secretary of State for War, St. John Brodrick, administered a rebuke typical of those Churchill was often to receive for daring to speak his mind without concern for party policy or discipline.

Those of us who disagree with him can only hope that the time will come when his judgment will grow up to his ability, when he will look back with regret to the day when he came down to the House to preach Imperialism without being willing to bear the burdens of Imperialism, and when the hereditary qualities he possesses of eloquence and courage may be tempered also by discarding the hereditary desire to run Imperialism on the cheap.

WILFRID SCAWEN BLUNT:
"A STRANGE REPLICA OF HIS FATHER" [4]

The complexities of Churchill's character were seen clearly by the anti-imperialist publicist Wilfrid Scawen Blunt, who met him in 1903.

He is a little, square-headed fellow of no very striking appearance, but of wit, intelligence, and originality. In mind and manner he is a strange replica of his father, with all his father's suddenness and assurance, and I should say more than his father's ability. There is just the same gaminerie and contempt of the conventional and the same engaging plain spokenness and readiness to understand. As I listened to him recounting conversations he had had with Chamberlain I seemed once more to be listening to Randolph on the subject of Northcote and Salisbury. About Chamberlain he was especially amusing, his attitude being one of mingled contempt and admiration, contempt for the man and admiration for his astuteness and audacity. In opposition Winston I expect to see playing precisely his father's game, and I should not be surprised if he had his father's success. He has a power of writing Randolph never had, who was a schoolboy with his pen, and he had education and a political tradition. He interested me immensely.

[4] Wilfrid Scawen Blunt, *My Diaries* (London, 1919-20), II, 488-89. Reprinted by permission of the Syndics of the Fitzwilliam Museum, Cambridge, England.

A. J. BALFOUR: ADVICE TO A YOUNG CRITIC [5]

In 1904 Churchill left the Conservative Party to become a Liberal. He at once turned even more savagely against Conservative policy, and denounced his former colleagues as the tools of outdated privilege and champions of social injustice. This stung the Conservative Prime Minister, A. J. Balfour, into a sharp reply.

As for the junior Member for Oldham his speech was certainly not remarkable for good taste, and as I have always taken an interest in that honourable gentleman's career, I should certainly, if I thought it in the least good, offer him some advice on that particular subject. But I take it that good taste is not a thing that can be acquired by industry, and that even advice of a most heartfelt and genuine description would entirely fail in effect if I were to offer it to him. But on another point I think I may give him some advice which may be useful to him in the course of what I hope will be a long and distinguished career. It is not, on the whole, desirable to come down to this House with invective which is both prepared and violent. The House will tolerate, and very rightly tolerate, almost anything within the rule of order which evidently springs from genuine indignation aroused by the collision of debate. But to come down with these prepared phrases is not usually successful, and at all events, I do not think it was very successful on the present occasion. If there is preparation there should be more finish, and if there is so much violence there should certainly be more veracity of feeling.

MAC CALLUM SCOTT: THE CHAMPION OF LIBERALISM [6]

By turning against the Conservatives, Churchill forfeited the sympathy of a large section of the Conservative Party.

[5] From *Hansard*, July 27, 1905. Reprinted by permission of the Controller of Her Majesty's Stationery Office. Readers should see Churchill's essay on Balfour in *Great Contemporaries* (London, 1937), pp. 237-57.

[6] From A. MacCallum Scott, *Winston Spencer Churchill* (London, 1905), pp. 262-63, 264-66. Reprinted by permission of J. MacCallum Scott. MacCallum Scott, who was the same age as Churchill, also wrote *Winston Churchill in War and Peace* (London, 1916). He subsequently served under Churchill as Parliamentary Private Secretary at the Ministry of War and Air, 1919.

Many refused to regard any of his notions except with hostility and suspicion, even after he returned to the Conservative Party in 1925. His twenty years as a Liberal could never be fully forgiven by a Party for which loyalty, however blind, was a prime principle. The Liberals, however, were fascinated by their new recruit, and in 1905 a Liberal MP, *MacCallum Scott, became Churchill's first biographer. Churchill was then only thirty.*

During the four years of his parliamentary career Churchill has not had many opportunities for developing a social programme. He came to Parliament without any previous political training or experience. He had to gather knowledge and skill as he went along from day to day. The immediate work which he found lying ready to his hand absorbed all his energies. The criticism of the Government's methods in South Africa, the advocacy of retrenchment, the attack on Mr. Brodrick's Army Reform Scheme, and the defence of Free Trade left him little time for more general political considerations. But he is on the right side. His sympathies are with labour as against the power of organised wealth. He is determined that capital shall be made the servant and not the master of the State. He believes that the true happiness of nations is to be secured by industrial development and social reform at home, rather than by territorial expansion and military adventures abroad. . . .

No one who has studied impartially the varied career and achievements of this young man can doubt that he was born to greatness. Wherever fortune has led him he has pressed forward to the very van. In every work to which he has put his hand he has excelled. He will ever be a leader, whether of a forlorn hope or of a great party. Already in the House of Commons he leads by a natural right which no man can dispute. He does the inevitable act which no one had thought of before; he thinks the original thought which is so simple and obvious when once it has been uttered; he coins the happy phrase which expresses what all men have longed to say, and which thereafter comes so aptly to every man's tongue. He is not simply a unit on one side or the other, and the transference of his vote counts for more than two on a division. He not only thinks, and feels, and speaks; he does, and the crowd who can only follow in beaten tracks do likewise.

With deliberate intention Churchill has singled out Mr. Chamberlain as the antagonist against whom he is to measure his strength in the immediate future. His candidature at Manchester is more than an attempt to find a seat in the next House of Commons. North West Manchester is but the platform from which he addresses the whole industrial north. He aims at no less than to throw Lancashire into the scale against Birmingham and the Midlands. "That is the policy of Birmingham," he said at the National Liberal Federation meeting, "and we are going to erect against that policy of Birmingham the policy of Manchester." He will revive the faded glories of the "Manchester school," raise aloft the tattered flag, and rally to his own person the dispersed forces of Free Trade in one long line of battle. It is a bold and ambitious idea, and the struggle will be a highly dramatic one. Will he win? Is he the destined man to bring back to Lancashire the political hegemony of the provinces? He plays for high stakes, but his nerve is steady and his eye is clear. He will at any rate make a fight for it, and the fight will be something to have lived for and to have seen.

THEODORE ROOSEVELT: A WARM DISLIKE [7]

Theodore Roosevelt had only met Churchill briefly on one occasion in 1901 shortly before Roosevelt assumed the Presidency of the United States. In 1906 he read Churchill's newly published biography of his father.

I have been over Winston Churchill's life of his father. I dislike the father and dislike the son, so I may be prejudiced. Still, I feel that, while the biographer and his subject possess some real farsightedness, especially in their appreciation of the shortcomings of that "Society" which had so long been dominant in English politics, and which produces in this country the missionary and the mug-

[7] Quoted in E. E. Morison, ed., *The Letters of Theodore Roosevelt* (Cambridge, Mass.: 1951-54), Vol. V, letter no. 4047, dated September 12, 1906. When war broke out in 1914 Roosevelt was told of Churchill's success at the Admiralty and wrote to his informant: "I have never liked Winston Churchill, but in view of what you tell me as to his admirable conduct and nerve in mobilizing the fleet, I do wish that if it comes in your way you would extend to him my congratulations on his action." Vol. VI, letter no. 5913, dated August 22, 1914. These two extracts are reprinted by permission of the Harvard University Press.

wump; yet they both possess or possessed such levity, lack of sobriety, lack of permanent principle, and an inordinate thirst for that cheap form of admiration which is given to notoriety, as to make them poor public servants.

A. G. GARDINER: "IN THE THICK OF THE FIGHT" [8]

In 1908 the journalist and essayist A. G. Gardiner published a perceptive essay about Churchill which was widely commented on at the time.

He is extraordinarily youthful even for his years. He has the curiosity and animation of a child—a child in fairyland, a child consumed with the thirst for life. He must know all, taste all, devour all. He is drunk with the wonder and the fascination of living. A talk with him is as exhilarating as a gallop across country, so full is it of adventure, and of the high spirits and eagerness of youth. No matter what the subject, soldiering or science, religion or literature, he plunges into it with the joy of a boy taking a "header" in the sea. And to the insatiable curiosity and the enthusiasm of the child he joins the frankness of the child. He has no reserves and no shams. He takes you, as it were, by the arm on the instant, and makes you free of all the domain of his mind. You are welcome to anything that he has, and may pry into any corner you like. He has that scorn of concealment that belongs to a caste which never doubts itself. And he is as frank with himself as with you. "Yes," he said, "I have read James' *Immortality*. I have read it three times. It impressed me deeply. But finally I came to the conclusion that I was lacking in the religious sense, and put it away."

His school was the barrack-room; his university the battle-field. He has served in two regiments of the line, fought with the Spaniards in Cuba, and held a commission in the South African Light Horse. He knows life in four continents, and has smelt powder in three. He has seen more wars than any man of his years; written more books than any soldier living. He has been a war correspondent; he has been taken prisoner; he has escaped from prison. And

[8] Quoted in A. G. Gardiner, *Prophets, Priests and Kings* (London, 1908), pp. 107-11. Reprinted by permission of J. M. Dent and Sons Ltd. Publishers. This passage should be compared with Gardiner's later assessment quoted on page 94 of this volume.

he showed the same address in war as in politics. General Smuts told me that when he held up the armoured train on which Mr. Churchill was captured he was struck by the energy and capacity of a fair-haired youth who led the defence. When they surrendered this youth modestly claimed special privileges in telegraphing to his friends on the ground that he was a war correspondent. The General laughed. "You have done all the damage that's been done," he said. "You fight too well to be treated as a civilian." "And now," added the General, in telling me the story, "I am going to the Colonial Office to see if I can get a favour out of that fair-haired youth in memory of our meeting on the veldt."

When, hot from campaigning on Indian frontiers and Egyptian sands, he galloped up to Westminster with his breezy "stand and deliver," he found Mr. Balfour lacking in enthusiasm. Mr. Balfour knew his father—indeed, followed his father in the jolly Hounslow Heath days of the early eighties. But while it was capital fun to go tiger-hunting with a Churchill, it was another affair to have a Churchill worrying you in office. He remembered his uncle's famous *mot*. When, after the memorable resignation, he was asked if he did not want Lord Randolph back, Lord Salisbury replied: "When you have got rid of a boil on the neck, you don't want it back again." Mr. Balfour determined that he would not have a boil on the neck.

His coolness did Mr. Churchill a service. It hastened his inevitable development. Like his father, he has the instinct of the democrat. His intellectual fearlessness carries him resistlessly along the path of constitutional development. The fundamental vice of Conservatism is that it distrusts the people. Its fundamental policy is to hoodwink the people, bribe them, drug them, use them as tools. Lord Randolph saw the folly of this. He saw that no party could be vital without the sanction of an instructed people, and that the modern State was healthy in proportion to the development of a healthy democratic opinion. He tried to hitch the democracy to the Tory chariot. It was a gallant dream, and he was broken on the wheel in the attempt. Mr. Churchill is happier in his fate. He was fired out of the Tory tabernacle before he had eaten out his heart in a vain service.

What of his future? At thirty-four he stands before the country the most interesting figure in politics, his life a crowded drama of action, his courage high, his vision unclouded, his boats burned. "I love Churchill, and trust him," said one of his colleagues to me. "He has the passion of democracy more than any man I know. But don't forget that the aristocrat is still there—latent and submerged, but there nevertheless. The occasion may come when the two Churchills will come into sharp conflict, and I should not like to prophesy the result." That danger seems remote. More than any man of his time, he approaches an issue without mental reserves and obscure motives and restraints. You see all the processes of his mind. It may be said of him, as Lord Russell said of the British Constitution, that he is like a hive of bees working under a glass cover. He leaves you in no doubt. He does not "hum and ha." He is not paralysed by the fear of consequences, nor afraid to contemplate great changes. He knows that to deal in millions is as simple as to deal in pence, and that timidity is the unpardonable sin of politics.

Has he staying power? Can one who has devoured life with such feverish haste retain his zest to the end of the feast? How will forty find him?—that fatal forty when the youth of roselight and romance has faded into the light of common day and the horizon of life has shrunk incalculably, and when the flagging spirit no longer answers to the spur of external things, but must find its motive and energy from within, or find them not at all.

That is the question that gives us pause. For, with all his rare qualities, Mr. Churchill is the type of "the gentleman of fortune." He is out for adventure. He follows politics as he would follow the hounds. He has no animus against the fox, but he wants to be in "at the kill." It is recorded that when, a fiery-headed boy at Harrow, he was asked what profession he thought of taking up, he replied, "The Army, of course, so long as there's any fighting to be had. When that's over, I shall have a shot at politics." He is still the Harrow boy, having his "shot at politics"—not so much concerned about who the enemy may be or about the merits of the quarrel as about being in the thick of the fight and having a good time. With the facility of the Churchill mind he feels the pulse of Liberalism with astonishing sureness, and interprets it with extraordinary ability. But the sense of high purpose is not yet apparent through the fierce joy of battle that possesses him. The passion for humanity, the stern resolve to see justice done though the heavens fall and he be buried in the ruins, the surrender of himself to the cause—these things have yet to come. His eye is less on the fixed stars than on the wayward meteors of the night. And when the exhilaration of youth is gone, and the gallop of high spirits has run its course, it may be that this deficiency of abiding and high compelling purpose will be a heavy handicap. Then it will be seen how far courage and intellectual address, a mind acutely responsive to noble impulses, and a quick and apprehensive political instinct will carry him in the leadership of men.

LORD RIDDELL: THE OTHER SIDE OF CHURCHILL [9]

Many English politicians tried to portray Churchill as a crude, intolerant, insincere person. But close friends, like the newspaper proprietor Lord Riddell, saw another side of his character.

For the past twelve months I have usually played golf with Winston twice a week. He is a charming companion, full of witty, amusing, unexpected sayings—never dull, never tedious. I find him a most considerate and loyal friend. He is also kind-hearted. The other day we came across a worm on the golf-course. Winston tenderly picked it up and placed it in the bracken, saying, "Poor fellow! If I leave you here, you will be trampled upon by some ruthless boot!"

THE NEW YORK WORLD: IN DEFENSE OF CHURCHILL [10]

Conservatives disliked Churchill's plans for a halt in the armaments race. The London Times portrayed him as lacking in the qualities of a warrior. It was left to the New York World to defend the principles of his actions.

A chorus of angry abuse is directed against Winston Churchill by the jingo press of Berlin because of his proposal that Germany

[9] From Lord Riddell, *More Pages from My Diary* (London, 1934), p. 24. Reprinted by permission of Country Life Limited. This volume is a rich source of stories about Churchill and reports of his conversation, as are its companion volumes, *War Diary* and *Intimate Diary of the Peace Conference and After.*
[10] From the New York *World*, March 30, 1913.

and Great Britain suspend naval construction for one year. To the
heated imagination of certain German jingoes the suggestion is a
"foul plot."

The First Lord of the Admiralty appealed openly to the common
sense and self interest of both nations. So far from being imprac-
ticable and Utopian, his offer is thoroughly practical. The only
sound pretext for either nation's spending tens of millions of dollars
every year on new armaments is that the other is doing the same
thing. In the end their relative strength on the sea is not changed.
Both are committed to a common folly—"Wasteful, purposeless
and futile folly," as Winston Churchill declared—and a preventable
folly. Why not stop it? Why not take a "naval holiday," if only
for one year?

That is precisely the kind of bargain that in his own affairs any
thinking man would welcome. He would save his money. He would
husband his resources. Why cannot two nations like Germany and
Great Britain be equally sane? Why should the offer of a "naval
holiday" be dangerous because it is reasonable? Do the greatest
powers of Europe propose to plead that they are bankrupt in intelligence as a preliminary to becoming financially bankrupt through
the folly of militarism?

H. H. ASQUITH: "HE WILL NEVER GET TO THE TOP" [11]

*The Liberal Prime Minister, H. H. Asquith, was a close
personal friend. His Government had gained a great deal from
Churchill's activities: much valuable progressive social legislation from 1906 to 1910 and a Navy alert and secure enough
to defend Britain against the combination of the German,
Austrian, and Turkish Empires.*

It is not easy to see what W[inston]'s career is going to be here.
He is to some extent blanketed by E. Grey and Ll. George, & has
no personal following: he is always hankering after coalitions and
odd regroupings, mainly designed (as one thinks) to bring in F. E.
Smith & perhaps the Duke of Marlborough. I think his future one
of the most puzzling enigmas in politics. . . .

[11] Quoted in Roy Jenkins, *Asquith* (London, 1964), pp. 339-40. Reprinted by
permission of the Chilmark Press Inc. Churchill's essay on Asquith in his volume
Great Contemporaries (London, 1937), pp. 137-51, should also be read.

It is a pity that Winston hasn't a better sense of proportion, and also a larger endowment of the instinct of loyalty. . . . I am really fond of him, but I regard his future with many misgivings. . . . He will never get to the top in English politics, with all his wonderful gifts; to speak with the tongue of men and angels, and to spend laborious days and nights in administration, is no good if a man does not inspire trust. . . .

His mouth waters at the sight and thought of K[itchener]'s new armies. Are these "glittering Commands" to be entrusted to "dugout trash," bred on the obsolete tactics of 25 years ago—"mediocrities, who have led a sheltered life mouldering in military routine" &c &c. For about ¼ of an hour he poured forth a ceaseless cataract of invective and appeal, & I much regretted that there was no shorthand writer within hearing—as some of his unpremeditated phrases were quite priceless. . . . He has now left to have a talk with Arthur Balfour, but will be back here at dinner. He is a wonderful creature, with a curious dash of schoolboy simplicity (quite unlike Edward Grey's), and what someone said of Genius—"A zigzag streak of lightning in the brain."

LORD HANKEY: CONFIDENCE AND ENERGY IN WAR [12]

Other politicians and Government servants observed Churchill during the war. Sir Maurice Hankey was Secretary to the Committee of Imperial Defence and to the War Council. He was a man privy to all Government secrets and undertook heavy responsibilities in both World Wars. Of Churchill in 1914 he later wrote:

Winston Churchill was a man of a totally different type from all his colleagues. He had a real zest for war. If war there must needs be, he at least could enjoy it. The sound of guns quickened his pulses, and he was one of those rare people who could, at the outset of the war at any rate, feel something of the *joie-de-bataille,* which even Jack Seely, one of the bravest men I ever knew, said could not survive a long-continued barrage of heavy shell and high explosive. Churchill's courage was an invaluable asset to the Cabinet,

[12] From Lord Hankey, *The Supreme Command, 1914-1918* (London, 1961), pp. 185-86. Reprinted by permission of George Allen and Unwin Ltd.

to Parliament, and to the nation in these early days. When all looked black and spirits were inclined to droop, he could not only see, but could compel others to see, the brighter side of the picture. The Navy did not offer sufficient scope for his unbounded energies. He must have an army too—and to this I had been urging him for years, for the exercise of sea-power often requires the co-operation of a small military force to carry out raids and diversions on the coast or to defend advanced bases from attack by land or sea. But the plan which he had adopted in a limited form, for creating such a force out of the Royal Marines, was not enough for him. He must have in addition a distinctive force: Churchill's Own. Hence the Naval Division into which so many brilliant young men were attracted and at Antwerp he showed that he wanted to use his own force in his own way. He brought an element of youth, energy, vitality and confidence that was a tower of strength to Asquith's Cabinet in those difficult early days.

DAVID LLOYD GEORGE: CHURCHILL IN ECLIPSE [13]

In May 1915, when Asquith formed a Coalition Government with both Liberal and Conservative Ministers, Churchill was forced out of the Admiralty by Conservative hostility. Churchill's exclusion from any important post—he was given the sinecure of Chancellor of the Duchy of Lancaster—was the ransom which Conservatives charged for entering the Government. Lloyd George, who became Minister of Munitions and whose political star was slowly rising, later defended Churchill's position at this time, and deplored his removal from high office.

The most notable change was the taking of Mr. Winston Churchill out of the Admiralty and placing him in charge of the Duchy of Lancaster, a post generally reserved either for beginners in the Cabinet or for distinguished politicians who had reached the first stages of unmistakable decrepitude. It was a cruel and unjust degradation. The Dardanelles failure was due not so much to Mr. Churchill's precipitancy as to Lord Kitchener's and Mr. Asquith's procrastination. Mr. Churchill's part in that unfortunate enterprise

[13] From *War Memoirs of David Lloyd George*, two volume edition (London, 1938), I, 139, 142. Reprinted by permission of the Beaverbrook Foundations.

had been worked out by him with the most meticulous care to the last particular, and nothing had been overlooked or neglected as far as the naval operations were concerned. The fatal delays and mishandlings had all been in the other branch of the Service. It is true that the conception of a one-sided Naval operation without simultaneous military action was due to Mr. Churchill's impetuosity, but both the Prime Minister and Lord Kitchener were equally convinced that it was the right course to pursue. When I learned the office finally offered to Mr. Churchill, it came to me as an unpleasant surprise. I reckoned it would have been impossible to keep him at the Admiralty, in view of the dispute which had precipitated the crisis. The Unionists would not, and could not in the circumstances, have assented to his retention in that office. But it was quite unnecessary in order to propitiate them to fling him from the masthead, whence he had been directing the fire, down to the lower deck to polish the brass. In the first sorting out and allotment of offices in which I had taken part, it had been arranged that he should be placed in the Colonial Office, where his energies would have been helpfully employed in organising our resources in the Empire beyond the seas; and I cannot to this hour explain the change of plans which suddenly occurred. The brutality of the fall stunned Mr. Churchill, and for a year or two of the War his fine brain was of no avail in helping in its prosecution.

ANDREW DEWAR GIBB: CHURCHILL AT THE FRONT [14]

In November 1915 Churchill gave up his sinecure position of Chancellor of the Duchy of Lancaster. Denied the power to influence the Government's war policy, he went to the trenches to play a humbler part as a Lieutenant Colonel commanding a small battalion. For six months he fought in the front line, facing German artillery bombardment and machine-gun fire each day. His Adjutant, Captain Dewar Gibb, described this little-known period of Churchill's life.

[14] From Captain X (pseudonym for Captain Andrew Dewar Gibb), *With Winston Churchill at the Front* (Glasgow, 1924), pp. 72-74, 109-11. Reprinted by permission of Nigel M. Dewar Gibb. Captain Gibb was subsequently Chairman of the Scottish National Party and Regius Professor of Law in the University of Glasgow.

It always struck me that Colonel Churchill achieved in a remarkable measure success in dealing with the rank and file of his battalion. His attitude towards the men was ideally sympathetic and was not marred by that condescending *hauteur* which goes so far to frustrate the efforts of a number of our regular officers. He found that the sentries were not as whole-hearted and enthusiastic in the performance of their watch as he desired and for many nights he made a particular point of explaining their duties to them, going along the front line and selecting positions for the men which at once gave a maximum of shelter and enabled them to keep a perfect look-out. To the young boys among them, especially, it seemed an unpleasant thing to stand up for an hour and expose oneself to the all too frequent bullets that came over to us from the German sentries. Winston used to get up on to the firestep and encourage them, demonstrating to them what a small chance, after all, there was of their being hit and pointing out too how vital were the duties which they were performing. In all this there was such a complete absence of the "superior person" that the men welcomed his presence and his advice, and responded most loyally to his orders. He held very strong views about the crime of "sleeping on his post" and was always at the utmost pains, in fairness to the men, to prevent the possibility of such a thing occurring.

No commanding officer ever was more interested in or more attentive to his wounded. On the one hand he was utterly impervious to all feelings of aversion from the unpleasant sights of war and I have seen him several times sitting calmly discussing questions of state with "Archie" in blood-saturated surroundings: but on the other he was always first on the scene of misfortune and did all in his power to help and comfort and cheer. It did not matter where he was or what he was doing, if he heard that a man was wounded he set off at once to see him.

I am firmly convinced that no more popular officer ever commanded troops. As a soldier he was hard-working, persevering and thorough. The expected fireworks never came off. He was out to work hard at tiresome but indispensable detail and to make his unit efficient in the very highest possible degree. I say nothing of his tactical and strategic ability—these were not tested in our time, but I cannot conceive that exceptionally creative and fertile brain failing in any sphere of human activity to which it was applied. And more-over, he loved soldiering: it lay very near his heart and I think he could have been a very great soldier. How often have we heard him say by way of encouragement in difficult circumstances, "War is a game to be played with a smiling face." And never was precept more consistently practised than this.

I speak with all possible warmth and affection of him as the friend of his officers. This was most strikingly demonstrated in the last days of his command when he was anxious to find employment, congenial employment, for those who were to be thrown out into the cold when the battalions amalgamated. He took endless trouble: he borrowed motor-cars and *scoured* France, interviewing Generals and Staff-officers great and small, in the effort to do something to help those who had served under him. Needless to say, the orderly-room was seething with applications of all sorts, possible and im-possible, but he treated them all with the utmost patience and good humour. No man was ever kinder to his subordinates and no commanding officer I have ever known was half so kind.

There is little more to be said. The early months of 1916 are by far my most treasured war-memory. It was my happiest time and it was my most interesting time. For work in intimate association with Winston Churchill was the last experience in the world any of us expected—our course did not lie that way. At first the prospect frightened us, but those feelings did not survive the first week. We came to realize, to realize at first hand, his transcendent ability. He came to be looked on as really a possession of our own, and one of which we were intensely proud. And much more, he became our friend. He is a man who apparently is always to have enemies. He made none in his old regiment, but left behind him there men who will always be his loyal partizans and admirers, and who are proud of having served in the Great War under the leadership of one who is beyond question a great man.

A. G. GARDINER: "KEEP YOUR EYE ON CHURCHILL" [15]

While Churchill was serving in Flanders and facing the many perils of trench warfare, A. G. Gardiner published a

[15] From A. G. Gardiner, *Pillars of Society* (London, 1916), pp. 152-58. Re-printed by permission of J. M. Dent and Sons Ltd., Publishers. This passage

*fascinating analysis of Churchill's character, which, although
in many ways extremely critical, was nevertheless a perceptive
and not entirely unfriendly review of his personality and pros-
pects. In spite of the range of his political experience, Churchill
was still only forty-two.*

He is the unknown factor in politics. You may cast the horo-
scope of anyone else; his you cannot cast. You cannot cast it because
his orbit is not governed by any known laws, but by attractions that
deflect his path hither and thither. It may be the attraction of war
or of peace, of social reform or of a social order—whatever it is he
will plunge into it with all the schoolboy intensity of his nature.
His loves may be many, but they will always have the passion of a
first love. Whatever shrine he worships at, he will be the most fervid
in his prayers.

He is the typical child of his time. It is a time of feverish activity,
of upheaval and challenge, of a world in revolt. The dams have
broken down and the waters are flooding the land. The old continents are submerged, and new and strange worlds are shaping
themselves before our eyes. In one of his letters, written during those
astonishing days when Chatham was sweeping the French out of
India with one hand and out of Canada with the other, Horace
Walpole said that on waking in the morning he was in the habit of
asking what new world had been conquered to-day? We might in
these times ask daily what ancient fabric has fallen, what venerable
tradition has been jettisoned, what new gospel has leapt into the
saddle. It is as if we are in a world that has awoke from a sleep and
has set out on a furious march with sealed orders. Labour is marching, the women are marching. Religion, politics, journalism, literature—all are seething with a new and unintelligible life. Harmony
has gone out of music and beauty out of art. The Ten Command-
ments are challenged and the exploitation of self is elevated into
a religion. Even Toryism is seized with the fever of action. Mr. Balfour stands aloof as the last standard-bearer of laissez-faire—the last
believer in the futility of human endeavour to shape the channels
of humanity. He is all reflection and no action. The new Toryism
is all action and no reflection. "Let us do something—never mind

should be compared with Gardiner's earlier comments of 1908, quoted on pages
84-87 of this volume.

what it is, but do it." The prophet of all this unrest is Bergson, who tells us that our minds are "orientated towards action rather than pure knowledge." Don't reflect: Act. That is the gospel.

Into this vast turmoil Mr. Churchill plunges with the joy of a man who has found his natural element. A world in transition is a world made for him. Life is a succession of splendid sensations, of thrilling experiences. He rushes from booth to booth with the delight of a boy at a fair. And each booth is more wonderful than any other. He must shoot at every gallery, shy at every cocoa-nut, see every bearded woman and two-headed man. He is reckless of his life and of his money, indifferent to consequences. All that matters is this magic world of which he has become the momentary possessor, and which he must devour ere the curtain is rung down on the drama and the dream.

With this abnormal thirst for sensation, he combines an unusual melodramatic instinct. He is always unconsciously playing a part —an heroic part. And he is himself his most astonished spectator. He sees himself moving through the smoke of battle—triumphant, terrible, his brow clothed with thunder, the legions looking to him for victory, and not looking in vain. He thinks of Napoleon; he thinks of his great ancestor. Thus did they bear themselves; thus, in this rugged and most awful crisis, will he bear himself. It is not make-believe, it is not insincerity: it is that in that fervid and pic- turesque imagination there are always great deeds afoot with him- self cast by destiny in the Agamemnon role. Hence that portentous gravity that sits on his youthful shoulders so oddly, those impressive postures and tremendous silences, the body flung wearily in the chair, the head resting gloomily in the hand, the abstracted look, the knitted brow. Hence that tendency to exaggerate a situation which is so characteristic of him—the tendency that sent artillery down to Sidney Street and, during the railway strike, despatched the military hither and thither as though Armageddon was upon us. "You've mistaken a coffee-stall row for the social revolution," said one of his colleagues to him as he pored with knitted and portentous brows over a huge map of the country on which he was marking his mili- tary dispositions. His mind once seized with an idea works with enormous velocity round it, intensifies it, enlarges it, makes it shadow the whole sky. In the theatre of that mind it is always the hour of fate and the crack of doom.

It is this impressionableness that makes him so vital and various.
He astonishes by his accomplishments. How, we ask, has one so
young, whose years have been years of breathless action, acquired
this large mastery of ideas, this power of statement, this grasp of
facts, this air of authority? It is not by application and industry
alone that he has succeeded, though he has these in an unusual
degree. He labours at a subject with the doggedness of Stonewall
Jackson. He polishes a speech as the lapidary polishes a stone. He
will have no loose ends, no unfortified assertions or slipshod phrases,
none of those unconsidered asides with which Mr. Lloyd George
invites attack. When after one of his speeches at Dundee a friend
of mine called on him on an important matter at one o'clock in
the morning, he found him sitting up in bed immersed in Blue
books. His father when Chancellor of the Exchequer asked, according to Sir Algernon West, the meaning of the decimal points, and
when told replied, "I've often wondered what those d—d dots
meant." Perhaps it was his fun; but he was certainly ignorant. Mr.
Churchill always knows what the dots mean.

But more potent than his industry is his astonishing apprehension.
He flashes through life taking impressions, swift, searching, detached. He absorbs a moral or an intellectual atmosphere as another
man absorbs the oxygen of the air, and he gives it out as if it were
his own vital breath. He is what the Spiritualists call a "medium"
—a vehicle through which some vision, some doctrine, some enthusiasm finds temporary utterance apart from himself. No one has
stated the principles of Liberalism with such breadth as he has done;
no one has preached peace with more fervour, economy with more
conviction, and social reform with a more thrilling break in the
voice; or, on the other hand, presented an unexampled naval expenditure with such an adroit and disarming appearance of sad
necessity. Each task, however subversive of former tasks, finds him
perfectly equipped, for he always knows his subject, and convinces
himself first. He is direct, rests his case on a plain argument, and
avoids all the dialectical cobwebs by which the Cecils delight the
intellect and bewilder the public. In saying this I do not wish to
exaggerate the importance of consistency. A pedantic consistency is
a sterile frame of mind. We all change if we are alive: we can all
say with Whitman:

Do I contradict myself?
Very well then, I contradict myself:
(I am large. I contain multitudes.)

It is not that Mr. Churchill is more multitudinous than others. It is that one seems to look in vain for that fundamental note that makes the discords of the supreme men plain. Ruskin was full of contradictions; but the ultimate Ruskin—the Ruskin with soul aflame for beauty and justice—emerges triumphant out of them all. It is the ultimate Churchill that escapes us. I think he escapes us for a good reason. He is not there.

In short, brilliantly as he preaches, he is the man of action simply, the soldier of fortune, who lives off adventure, loves the fight more than the cause, more even than his ambition or his life. He has one purpose—to be in the firing line, in the battles either of war or peace. If he cannot be there in one capacity he will be there in another. When the Cuban war broke out he got leave from his regiment, went out as a newspaper correspondent, and fought as a soldier. When the Malakand rising took place, his regiment not being engaged, he again got leave, again took service as a correspondent, again fought as a soldier, and got mentioned in the despatch for "courage and resolution at a critical moment." Back from the Tirah expedition, in which he had got himself appointed orderly officer to Sir William Lockhart, he went straight to the War Office and begged to be sent out with the expedition to the Soudan. Thence he returned to fight Oldham, missed it, and plunged into the South African War. That over, he galloped up to Westminster to "have his shot at politics." Never has there been such hustle. At twenty-five he had fought in more continents than any soldier in history save Napoleon, and seen as many campaigns as any living general.

Nor is it purposeless hustle. It always has a strict business basis. When in the Soudan he was attached to the 21st Lancers—known, I believe, as the "Saucy Devils"—there was resentment against this precocious intruder. Instead of giving him a troop to lead they put him in charge of the mess store, and one has described how he met him one day in charge of a decrepit mule and two donkeys. "Look at that. There is a trust for a British officer. It is not even a job for a noncommissioned officer. They have said, 'We'll break young Churchill's heart if he comes to us.' Poor little men! They think I'm as small as they are. But it's my object to write a big book on this campaign, and as long as I get up I don't mind in what capacity they employ me. Even if they give me a sweeper's job I should not demur." It is a fine story—as fine in its way, given the inferiority of motive, as that of Lincoln when General McClellan, according to his rude habit, had kept the President waiting for him. Someone expressed anger at the indignity. "Never mind," said Lincoln, "I will hold McClellan's horse if he will only bring us success."

It is more difficult for a Churchill than for a Lincoln to pocket his pride; humiliation no more than danger can check him, and the boy of twenty-three produced in *The River War* not merely the best history of the campaign, but one of the best military books in the language, a book, moreover, that in its attack on Lord Kitchener for the desecration of the Mahdi's body illustrated the courage, physical and moral, that is so conspicuous a virtue of Mr. Churchill. He is never afraid to risk his life. He showed that in his defence of the armoured train, but not less in the circumstances of his visit to Birmingham in the most feverish fiscal days. The howling crowd had assembled round the Town Hall to deal with him perhaps as they had dealt with Lloyd George. Lord Robert Cecil, who was to speak with him, went to the hall unobserved on foot, accompanied by a plain-clothes detective. Not so Mr. Churchill. Suddenly a carriage and pair drove into the midst of the hostile crowd. It contained only Mr. Churchill; open, palpable, flagrant; a challenge that might mean lynching. For a moment there was a pause: then the crowd, captured by the spirit of the thing, burst into cheers. It was another triumph for the Churchill audacity—that union of recklessness and calculation that snatches victory out of the jaws of danger.

And he had not only courage but the will to discipline himself and to triumph over grave defects. His appearance and his utterance are against him. There is still no better pen picture of him than that which the Boers issued in the warrant for his arrest after his escape from Pretoria: "Englishman, twenty-five years old, about 5ft 8ins. high, indifferent build, walks with a bend forward, pale appearance, red-brownish hair, small moustache hardly perceptible, talks through the nose and cannot pronounce the letter 's' properly." It is not a flattering picture. That defect of speech alone would have destroyed most men. Mr. Churchill makes you forget it by the sheer energy of his mind and manner. He rides, as it were, roughshod over himself. And so with his temperament. His natural habit is ebullient and provocative. He used to be rude and defiant: he has changed all that. He has become as discreet as a family lawyer, as decorous as a churchwarden. The spirit is still there, but it is curbed and bridled and obedient to its imperious master. He cultivates silence. And his silence is not less eloquent than his speech and far more significant. It is not an accident, for, with all his impulsiveness, nothing is accidental about this remarkable man. Behind all his actions, however sudden or headlong, there is the calculation of a singularly daring and far-sighted mind—a mind that surveys the field with the eye of the strategist, weighs the forces, estimates the positions and, when the hour has come, strikes with deadly sureness at the vulnerable place. "Keep your eye on Churchill" should be the watchword of these days. Remember, he is a soldier first, last and always. He will write his name big on our future. Let us take care he does not write it in blood.

DAVID LLOYD GEORGE: CONSERVATIVES COULD NOT FORGIVE [16]

In December 1916 Lloyd George became Prime Minister. As an admirer of Churchill's energy and vision, he wished to bring him back into the Coalition Government, but Conservative hostility was still too strong even for the persuasive Lloyd George.

The third ex-Minister who would have been helpful in Council was Mr. Winston Churchill—one of the most remarkable and puzzling enigmas of his time. When I took office he had ceased to be a Minister for some months, but he was still a prominent member of the Liberal Party. His fertile mind, his undoubted courage, his untiring industry, and his thorough study of the art of war, would have made him a useful member of a War Cabinet. Here his more erratic impulses could have been kept under control and his judg-

[16] From *The War Memoirs of David Lloyd George*, two volume edition (London, 1938), I, 635-38. Reprinted by permission of the Beaverbrook Foundations.

ment supervised and checked, before plunging into action. Men of his ardent temperament and powerful mentality need exceptionally strong brakes. Unfortunately, the Tory Ministers, with the exception of Mr. Balfour and Sir Edward Carson, were unanimous in their resolve that he should not be a member of the Ministry, and most of them made it a condition precedent to their entry into the Government that he should be excluded.

Mr. Bonar Law [Leader of the Conservative Party] had a profound distrust of him. I did my best to persuade him to withdraw his objection and I urged the argument which is usually advanced on these occasions, that Mr. Churchill would be more dangerous as a critic than as a Member of the Government. I remember saying to him that when I was practising as a solicitor one of my most responsible duties was the choice of Counsel in an important case. There was the type of man whom you could always depend upon to do his best for the client—and his best was of the very best at the Bar. On the other hand, there was the man of brilliant parts who on his day was even more formidable. His judgment, however, could never be quite depended upon. He was apt either in cross-examination or in speech to be guilty of an indiscretion which would ruin his client's chances. The difficulty in regard to him always was that if you left him out of your team, the other side might brief him and get the benefit of one of his reliable exhibitions of talent, and then I said the question one always had to put to oneself was this: "Is he more dangerous when he is FOR YOU than when he is AGAINST YOU?" When I put it in this way to Mr. Bonar Law, his reply was: "I would rather have him against us every time."

I deeply regretted this attitude, but I could not risk a break up of the political combination which was an essential foundation of the Government, for the sake of an immediate inclusion of Mr. Churchill in the Ministry. A few months later I was able to appoint him to the headship of the Ministry of Munitions. Even then the Tory antipathy to him was so great that for a short while the very existence of the Government was in jeopardy.

Here are some samples of the objections advanced at that later time by my colleagues. One of them wrote:—

> May I again and for the last time urge you to think well before you make the appointment (W.Ch.) which we have more than once

discussed? It will be an appointment intensely unpopular with many of your chief colleagues—in the opinion of some of whom it will lead to the disruption of the Government at an early date, even if it does not lead, as it may well do, to resignations now. X—who opened the subject to me of his own accord this evening and who has spoken to you, tells me that it will be intensely unpopular in the Army.

I have every reason to believe the same of the Navy. . . .

He is a potential danger in opposition. In the opinion of all of us he will as a member of the Government be an active danger in our midst.

Another Minister wrote at the same time: "Apart from every other consideration, is it wise for you to have as one of your Ministers, a dangerously ambitious man? . . ." And another important Conservative Minister wrote to me in similar strain:—"As regards W. Churchill and the Government, I have made enquiries and from what Z— tells me I am satisfied it would bring about a very grave situation in our Party. . . ."

Why were they so bitter and implacable? His political record naturally exasperated his old Party. He does nothing by halves, and when he left it he attacked his old associates and condemned his old principles with a vigour and a witty scorn which rankled. When War was declared the national peril constrained all parties into a temporary truce, in which party ranks and party rancours were for the time being overlooked or ignored. But Conservatives could not forgive nor forget Churchill's desertion to their enemies, and his brisk and deadly firing into their ranks at a moment when their rout had begun. Had he remained a faithful son of the political household in which he was born and brought up, his share in the Dardanelles fiasco would have been passed over and another sacrifice would have been offered up to appease the popular anger. There was an abundant choice from which the altar could have been supplied. His mistakes gave resentful Tories an irresistible opportunity for punishing rank treason to their party, and the lash which drove Churchill out of office, although knotted with the insults he had hurled at them, was wielded with an appearance of being applied not by vindictive partisans but by dutiful patriots.

For days I discussed with one or other of my colleagues Churchill, his gifts, his shortcomings, his mistakes, especially the latter. Some of them were more excited about his appointment than about the War. It was a serious crisis. It was interesting to observe in a concentrated form every phrase of the distrust and trepidation with which mediocrity views genius at close quarters. Unfortunately, genius always provides its critics with material for censure—it always has and always will. Churchill is certainly no exception to this rule.

They admitted he was a man of dazzling talents, that he possessed a forceful and a fascinating personality. They recognised his courage and that he was an indefatigable worker. But they asked why, in spite of that, although he had more admirers, he had fewer followers than any prominent public man in Britain? They pointed to the fact that at the lowest ebb of their fortunes, Joseph Chamberlain in Birmingham and Campbell-Bannerman in Scotland could count on a territorial loyalty which was unshakable in its devotion. On the other hand, Churchill had never attracted, he had certainly never retained, the affection of any section, province or town. His changes of Party were not entirely responsible for this. Some of the greatest figures in British political life had ended in a different Party from that in which they commenced their political career. That was therefore not an adequate explanation of his position in public confidence. They asked: What then was the reason?

Here was their explanation. His mind was a powerful machine, but there lay hidden in its material or its make-up some obscure defect which prevented it from always running true. They could not tell what it was. When the mechanism went wrong, its very power made the action disastrous, not only to himself but to the causes in which he was engaged and the men with whom he was co-operating. That was why the latter were nervous in his partnership. He had in their opinion revealed some tragic flaw in the metal. This was urged by Churchill's critics as a reason for not utilising his great abilities at this juncture. They thought of him not as a contribution to the common stock of activities and ideas in the hour of danger, but as a further danger to be guarded against.

I took a different view of his possibilities. I felt that his resourceful mind and his tireless energy would be invaluable under supervision. That he had vision and imagination, no one could doubt. The Dardanelles idea (apart from its execution), and his early discernment of the value of tanks clearly demonstrated his possession of these faculties. Men with such gifts are rare—very rare. In an emergency they ought to be utilised to the full, and if you keep a vigilant eye on their activities, they are a greater asset than a legion of the conventional sort.

That is why I thought he ought to be employed. I knew something of the feeling against him amongst his old Conservative friends, and that I would run great risks in promoting Churchill to any position in the Ministry; but the insensate fury they displayed when later on the rumour of my intention reached their ears surpassed all my apprehensions, and for some days it swelled to the dimensions of a grave ministerial crisis which threatened the life of the Government. I took the risk, and although I had occasionally some reason to regret my trust I am convinced I was right to overrule the misgivings of my colleagues, for Churchill rendered conspicuous service in further increasing the output of munitions when an overwhelming supply was essential to victory. As to Churchill's future, it will depend on whether he can establish a reputation for prudence without losing audacity.

BLACKWOOD'S MAGAZINE: THE DOG HAS HIS DAY [17]

In July 1917 Lloyd George finally persuaded his Conservative allies to allow Churchill to become Minister of Munitions. But they refused to contemplate his inclusion in the War Cabinet. He was allowed to manufacture weapons of war, but not to decide on major items of war policy. Even his tightly restricted sphere of activities came under attack from Conservative opinion, and the following anonymous article in Blackwood's Magazine *of September 1917 was typical of many.*

Mr. Winston Churchill is to-day Minister of Munitions. Having been discarded by Mr. Asquith, he is warmly embraced by Mr. Lloyd George, and his ill-omened return to power and influence is

---

[17] From an anonymous article, "Mr. Winston Churchill," published in *Blackwood's Magazine* (September 1917), pp. 397-407. The author was Charles Whibley, the essayist and literary critic. Reprinted by permission of William Blackwood and Sons Ltd., Publishers and Printers, of Edinburgh and London. After Churchill's death, *Blackwood's Magazine* (March 1965) contained an article on Churchill which reversed its earlier verdict. He understood, it said, "that despite the glitter of its panoply, war is grim and horrible."

another proof that our political system aims not at the welfare of
the country, but at the aggrandisement of the demagogue. The
career of Mr. Churchill is plain for all to see. He has held no office
that he has not discredited. Had he followed any other trade than
that of politics he would have been forced by his past into perpetual
retirement. But the politician is tried by an easier standard than
that which obtains in common life. And the greatest of Mr. Churchill's failures or misdemeanours is not enough to exclude him from
the councils of the nation. As we have said, he is Minister of Munitions to-day. It will be surprising if to-morrow he does not wriggle,
by the methods familiar to him and to us, into the narrow circle of
the War Cabinet.

When that eminent statesman, Sir Henry Campbell-Bannerman,
became, by the simple process of seniority, Prime Minister of England, Mr. Churchill was a new and zealous convert to the doctrines
of radicalism. There is no reason why he should not have changed
his opinions. As a dog is entitled to his bite, so a politician is permitted to rat—once. If he attempts to repeat the adventure, he is
looked upon, justly, with suspicion, and there is some comfort in the
reflection that Mr. Churchill will be left waving the red flag of
parochialism until the end of his life. Nor did he disappoint those
whom he had left. No sooner had he joined his new friends than he
displayed all the blatant energy of a convert. . . .

As Mr. Bonar Law said of him, who is now his colleague, Mr.
Churchill "has had a comparatively short public career, but it has
been varied, and perhaps you think it impossible that he can have
any surprise in store for us. You are mistaken. There is still a surprise that he might give us. It would stagger humanity. I really
thought it was coming. The thunderbolt will come when . . . the
First Lord of the Admiralty shows that he is ready on any question
to sacrifice his ambition to his convictions."

Mr. Churchill did not sacrifice his ambition to his convictions. . . .

We do not pretend to understand Mr. Churchill's presence in
the Government. The processes of politics are too deep for us. Obviously he was not selected because he was the best man for the place.
His mischievous past cannot be lightly overlooked, and he knows
nothing of the department which he is asked to control. "Well,"
said one of his hecklers at Dundee, "when some of us take on a job

we are supposed to know something about it." Politicians are exempted from the rules of knowledge and common sense, and there is no reason why a man should not be Chancellor of the Exchequer who cannot do a plain sum in addition. It is therefore not as an expert but as a mere politician that Mr. Churchill is permitted once more to interfere in the affairs of the Empire, and his appointment can be justified on no other plea than that—which is no plea at all —of political intrigue. Mr. Lloyd George said the other day, with perfect truth, that unity was essential in this crisis of the war. He will not promote unity by retrieving a pack of demagogues whom the whole country distrusts.

LORD BEAVERBROOK: "A FOOT IN BOTH CAMPS" [18]

Only when the war ended did Churchill enter the Cabinet, as Secretary of State for War and Air. Again the Conservative press, led by The Times, *was hostile. Lord Beaverbrook, the Canadian millionaire who had been British Minister of Information toward the end of the war, has sympathetically portrayed Churchill's dilemma immediately after the war.*

I have a picture of Churchill in my mind striding up and down in his room at the War Office, tingling with vitality. Bold and imaginative in the sweep of his conceptions, prolific of new ideas, like a machine gun of bullets and expelling his notions in much the same manner. Fertile, resourceful, courageous, he was always tolerant, though in this age occasionally wanting in prudence.

The political front was of course in confusion. There were days of broken lights of political faith. Was he nearer to Asquith's brand of Liberalism or did he freely accept Lloyd George and the Coalition? Was he a Liberal or a Tory?

He did not know himself.

Surely he had a foot in both camps. Not intentionally, but none

[18] From Lord Beaverbrook, *Men and Power, 1917-1918* (London, 1956), pp. 142-43. Reprinted by permission of the Beaverbrook Foundations. Churchill figures prominently in two other books by Beaverbrook, *Politicians and the War* (London, 1928) and *The Decline and Fall of Lloyd George* (London, 1963). The complex and at times stormy relationship between the two men is discussed in Kenneth Young, *Churchill and Beaverbrook* (London, 1965).

the less, what he did abroad pleased the Tories and infuriated the Radicals. When he spoke at home, he was cheered by Radicals, and how he annoyed the Tories!

It was not inconvenient to be in a position which permitted him to step off with either foot.

He talked brilliantly and with all the ardour of middle age. Some persons said he talked too much. He never surrounded himself with those who were only good listeners. His conversation was best when he spoke with a trusted companion.

Although he had not attained to his great prestige, he was apt even then to hold sway in a large gathering, acting all the time. He was a fine actor. And occasionally he indulged in mimicry of the speech of certain of his colleagues.

He drew from his well of experience. He differed from many of his political contemporaries who had a stock of stories frequently repeated. He was always truthful. He could keep a secret.

Here I leave him. All the years of the First War may be regarded as a schooling in strategy and in politics equipping Winston Spencer Churchill as the Master Mind of the world war as yet far, far distant.

H. G. WELLS: "I WANT TO SEE HIM OUT" [19]

Critics such as the novelist H. G. Wells, the socialist Fenner Brockway, and the journalist Victor Germains portrayed Churchill as a danger to his country and to any political party that trusted him. He was strongly believed to relish the very thought of war. Actually, at this time, he was actively engaged in seeking to reduce British military commitments, and to bring about a peaceful settlement both in Ireland and Turkey. But many of his fellow countrymen neither knew nor indeed cared to know of his abilities as a peacemaker. They used him as a symbol of all that was most ugly and aggressive in British life. H. G. Wells wrote:

[19] From an article by H. G. Wells published in the *Sunday Express,* December 12, 1920. Reprinted by permission of the Executors of H. G. Wells and with the agreement of the *Sunday Express.* Wells also expressed his hostility to Churchill in his novel *Men Like Gods* (London, 1923), where Churchill appears as Rupert Catskill, a warmonger whose "violent imaginations have caused the deaths of thousands of people."

I cannot call myself Anti-Churchill. I have known Mr. Churchill for a dozen years perhaps, and there is much to like in him. He has an imaginative liveliness rare in politicians, and his personality is unusually amusing. But I will confess that it distresses me that he should hold any public office at the present time. These are years of great scarcity, and Mr. Churchill is temperamentally a waster; there are dangerous corners ahead, and for two years Mr. Churchill has— if I may use the most expressive word—monkeyed with our Eastern policy. I want to see him out of any position of public responsibility whatever. I believe the estimate I have given of him here differs only in its frankness from the general estimate. His presence in the Government taints his colleagues and the Prime Minister with a flavour of cynicism.

The general public does not believe that they believe in him to any extent that justifies this association. The Government would look more serious and statesmanlike without him. And the retirement of Mr. Churchill would not be a tragic fall such as was Lord Haldane's, for example. Mr. Churchill has many resources. He would, for instance, be a brilliant painter.

FENNER BROCKWAY: "A PUBLIC DANGER AND A MENACE TO PEACE" [20]

The Independent Labour Party candidate Fenner Brockway said in his election address of 1924:

Mr. Churchill has previously charged Labour with setting class against class. It is he who is now the chief exponent of a class war. He raised the bogy of Socialism, and seeks to combine all the selfish and vested interest who fear the onward march of Labour.

[20] Quoted in Martin Gilbert, *Plough My Own Furrow* (The Story of Lord Allen of Hurtwood) (London, 1965), p. 176. Reprinted by permission of Lord Brockway. Forty-three years later Brockway, who had entered the House of Lords in 1964 after a long parliamentary career distinguished for its outspoken championship of the underdog, wrote:
"Looking back, I think this was an accurate picture of Winston Churchill's contribution to politics at that time. He had been a turn-about. He began as a Liberal, moved to the Left and became almost a Socialist, advocating the public ownership of essential services, swept again to the Right, hesitated between Liberalism and Conservatism (which stage he had reached by the time of my 1924 election address), then he joined the Conservatives and went to the

Three years ago Mr. Churchill described Labour as unfit to
govern. . . . In two months the Labour Government has achieved
for social betterment and peace more than any other Government
has achieved in as many years.

Of all the politicians Mr. Churchill has shown himself most unfit
for the responsibility of government. His forte is to be a disturber of
peace, whether at home or abroad. He is a political adventurer, with
a genius for acts of mischievous irresponsibility. He is militant to
the finger-tips . . . his use of troops during the railway dispute of
1911 and his wicked and wasteful expenditure of 100 millions of
British money in futile military attacks on Russia, prove how fatal
it would be to place him in a position of influence at a time when
the shattered world left by the war needs a healing hand of reconciliation. . . .

Mr. Churchill's record shows him to be a public danger and a
menace to the peace of the world.

He challenges our Socialism. We accept the challenge. Socialism
is not the destructive force in society which he denounces. It is the
one great constructive force.

It is not Socialism which is responsible for industrial unrest and
the class war. It is the want of Socialism. The cause is to be found in
the appalling difference in modern society between undeserved
poverty and undeserved riches, in the wretched existence of insecurity and semi-starvation to which thousands of workers are condemned by the existing system of civilization.

VICTOR GERMAINS: A BRILLIANT FAILURE [21]

*Victor Germains' biography was written in 1931, when
Churchill entered the political wilderness for the second time
in his life. Socialists still regarded him as a menace to social*

extreme Right. This record was obliterated by his premiership during the Second
World War when in a quite extraordinary way he served as the voice of the
nation and showed great breadth of view in his opposition to Hitler and Nazism
by his co-operation with Soviet Russia in the common cause. He was unique in
reflecting the Dunkirk spirit. Unhappily after the War he became the inspiration, in his Fulton speech in America, of the early British and later Dulles
American policy to isolate Soviet Russia. We are recovering from that, and now
it is perhaps better to remember what he did in war time against Nazism."
(Letter to the Editor, March 23, 1967.)

[21] From Victor Wallace Germains, *The Tragedy of Winston Churchill* (London,
1931), pp. 277-80. Reprinted by permission of The Hutchinson Group Ltd.

peace, Liberals as a traitor to their cause, and Conservatives as a troublemaker who could bring their Party nothing but anxiety and confusion.

If there was anyone who seemed foredained to end a war crowned with laurels and a natural successor to Mr. Asquith as Prime Minister of England, that man in 1914 seemed to be Mr. Winston Churchill. Yet for lack of the right balance of cool-headedness and judgement, all these advantages were thrown away. It was Mr. Lloyd George—who had been very half-hearted about declaring war on Germany—with all his record of Pacifism and Little Englandism behind him, who became the idol of the War-Party; it was Mr. Baldwin who became the chief agent in overthrowing Mr. Lloyd George; and it was Mr. Ramsay MacDonald—who throughout the War had been a convinced and determined Pacifist—who profited by the swing of the pendulum and who has twice held the prize for which Mr. Churchill secretly longs, the honour of being the King's first servant and the dominating voice in the councils of the world's greatest empire. What *has* been Mr. Churchill's career in reality but the tragedy of the brilliant failure, who has repeatedly seen men whom he secretly despises pass him on the road to office and power?

What is to be Winston Churchill's future? Will he reach his real goal, which is to be Prime Minister? One feels doubtful. What has he truly got to offer *any* party? Is he to preach Socialism or Liberalism in opposition to Ramsay MacDonald or Mr. Lloyd George? This is a game at which they can beat him hollow. Is he to *attack* Pacifism or Liberalism?

Think of the crushing retorts to which he will expose himself— and particularly from his erstwhile friend and colleague, the silver-tongued David from Wales. As a speaker—and at best—Winston Churchill is no real match for Mr. Lloyd George. Imagine the diabolical glee with which the Arch-Priest of Limehouse would turn Mr. Churchill's *own* former phrases against him. Is it to be a matter of flag-waving? Imperialism? Can Mr. Winston Churchill compete with Lords Beaverbrook or Rothermere in this respect?

But the true tragedy of Mr. Churchill is that whilst he has in reality nothing to *offer* the genuine Labour man, or Liberal, he fails to command the confidence of the genuine Conservative. For the ghosts of the Gallipoli dead will always rise up to damn him anew in times of national emergency. Neither official historians, nor military hack writers, will ever explain away or wipe out the memories of the Dardanelles.

What sensible man is going to place confidence in Mr. Churchill in any situation which needs cool-headedness, moderation, or tact? The present writer, speaking to one of the Right Honourable Gentleman's most enthusiastic admirers, posed the question point-blank: What would have happened in the last General Strike had Winston Churchill been a Conservative Prime Minister? The answer came unhesitatingly: *The streets would have run with blood.* Mr. Churchill in such a crisis would have been like a red rag to the Labour men, without being a source of moral strength to the Conservatives.

In this sense of latent distrust is to be found the greatest obstacle to the realization of Mr. Churchill's own most coveted ambition. The public looks upon him as a brilliant man but rash, hot-headed, impulsive.

One sometimes feels that at Mr. Winston Churchill's birth all the good fairies came trooping each with her guerdon: Imagination, Daring, Energy, *Guts,* each laid her gifts at the wonder-child's feet and went curtseying away. Then came those grim old fairies, Patience, Concentration, whom nobody had thought of inviting, and muddled all the other gifts up together so that the wonderful child grew up always in a desperate hurry and never able to tackle one particular job at a time, and to do this *thoroughly.*

Thus there developed an arch-apostle of the "short-cut" in politics as in war and the "short-cut" is something which must be used very judiciously, otherwise it may be the longest way round. It was the Tragedy of Winston Churchill that he never grasped this. Think of him in the plight of Cortes. Would he have reached Mexico and have conquered Montezuma and have triumphed not alone over the Aztecs but against the treachery and intrigues of his own followers? Winston Churchill would have had no lack of courage and tenacity, but he *would* have lacked the patience and cool-headedness of Cortes, and lacking these qualities would have made a fiasco of the whole business and then have come to the Court of Madrid with a long and eloquent story telling of the intrigues, treacheries and half-heartedness of his followers and attributing failure to this.

Anyone reading *The World-Crisis* would believe that none of the Great Captains of History had ever had to cope with half-hearted colleagues, Marlborough had not to face the vacillations of the Dutch; Nelson had not to cope with maladministration and jealousies; Wellington had no need for tact and patience in dealing with the Spanish. The real test of a man's character is that he surmounts his difficulties and not that he succumbs to these.

"The fault, dear Brutus, is not in our stars but in ourselves."

Winston Churchill, in his long and eloquent story to explain disaster, forgets all the *advantages* with which he started, advantages which would have made a Nelson or a Wellington sick with envy. A young man, with the vast and complex mechanism of the world's mightiest fleet at his disposal, a personal friend of the Prime Minister, the ægis of the powerful Liberal Party behind him, and the unstinted support which the British people give to their Navy—he threw all these gifts away in sheer headstrong recklessness; he lost himself trying a "short-cut" in unfamiliar territory, and he lost others with him.

If Mr. Lloyd George, with his undoubted genius as a speaker and his "feel" on the popular pulse, ended by smashing the Liberal Party, what is likely to happen to the Conservative Party under leadership of a Winston Churchill?

"Cleverness" and "wisdom" are not synonymous terms; there is still a broad gulf between the "man of talents" and the "man of genius." One may perhaps feel that at the present time when the Empire is going through the most terrible economic crisis known to history, the facile phrases, glittering hopes, and unbalanced enthusiasm, which issued in the Tragedy of the Dardanelles, are a little out of place—they may too easily eventuate in consequences irreparable, disastrous, and appalling.

LORD BIRKENHEAD: "THE FORCE OF SHEER GENIUS" [23]

Churchill had few supporters between the wars. Conservatives distrusted him, the Labour Party feared him, the pacifists thought him too warlike, the bellicose considered him too sentimental. The six observers whose remarks now follow were

[23] From Lord Birkenhead, *Contemporary Personalities* (London, 1924), pp. 114-15 and 118-23. Reprinted by permission of the 2nd Earl of Birkenhead, who wrote to the editor on March 23, 1967: "My father was probably Churchill's

*from very different walks of life. They were in a minority in
their appreciations of Churchill, but they saw the complexities
and attractions of his personality and his beliefs with greater
clarity than most. Lord Birkenhead, who had been a distinguished Conservative Lord Chancellor and brilliant lawyer,
was one of Churchill's closest friends.*

To those who know him well it is very remarkable how complete is the public misconception of the man. He is looked upon
as reserved, insolent, and even domineering. For these illusions his
own demeanour is (unintentionally) much to blame. He has no small
talk; and says everything which comes into his mind. Sometimes
caustic and disagreeable things come into it, though in private life
this very seldom happens. He walks through the Lobbies of the
House of Commons with an air appropriate to Napoleon Bonaparte
on the morning of the crisis of the 18th Brumaire. He does not mean
to be either reserved or rude; but he contrives to give the impression to those who know him little that he does not desire to know
them more. Only his friends understand him well. And they know
that there is no man in public life in England with a heart so warm,
with a simplicity so complete, with a loyalty so unswerving and so
dependable. He has, indeed, in the intimacy of personal friendship
a quality which is almost feminine in its caressing charm. And he
has never in all his life failed a friend, however embarrassing the
obligations, which he felt it necessary to honour, proved at the moment when he honoured them.

There is about him a simplicity which no other public man of
the highest distinction possesses. Lord Morley said of Lord Randolph Churchill that if you educated him you would ruin him.
Winston's education has been extremely partial, but he has attained
by the force of sheer genius to a mental equipment more complete
than most Senior Wranglers and most Heads of Colleges. It is

---

greatest friend but was never in any way dazzled by him, although having a
great respect for his gifts, and the fact that he was his intellectual equal, and
in some ways superior, makes his estimate of Churchill all the more valuable."
The 2nd Earl of Birkenhead is the author of *Halifax* (London, 1965), the
biography of the former Viceroy and Foreign Secretary, and of the biography
of his father, *Frederick Edwin Earl of Birkenhead* (London, 1933), both of which
contain important references to Churchill. See also Churchill's essay on Birkenhead in *Great Contemporaries* (London, 1937), pp. 171-83.

reported of him, and I believe truly, that a friend once lent him Welldon's translation of Aristotle's "Ethics," with a particular request that he should carefully study what that friend (rightly or wrongly) believed to be the greatest book in the world. Winston read it (or read part of it) and is reported to have said that he thought it very good. "But," he added, "it is extraordinary how much of it I had already thought out for myself."

It may not unplausibly be retorted that the war found him First Lord of the Admiralty, with a reasonable prospect of being the greatest War Minister in history before it ended. Everything smiled upon him in August, 1914. He became a popular figure; and many of the shrewdest judges of political forces predicted that he must emerge from the war recalling and repeating the triumphs of Chatham. But surely some malignant godmother, quarrelling with the shining gifts given to this astonishing child, must have added a discordant note of malevolence at his birth. His work at the Admiralty and his general conception of the strategy of the war were alike admirable.

But his able, restless, ambitious temperament was hardly content with its own legitimate ambit. He saw too much, and he tried to do too much. No one department, hardly one war, was enough for him in that sublime and meteoric moment. His fundamental conceptions were sound and even brilliant; but they marched too far in front of the material resources which even he could command. He was right about Antwerp; he took great personal risks to make the Antwerp policy successful; but it was doomed to failure before the attempt was made. His conception of the Dardanelles adventure was daring, brilliant and masterly. If successful, the attack, as he conceived it, would have shortened the war by two years; there would probably have been no Revolution in Russia and no Bolshevism, with all which this would have meant to the civilisation of Europe and to the security of the world.

And had he only been supreme with the uncontrolled power of appropriating from the Western front what was necessary—and it was so little—to make the Dardanelles campaign a certain success, he would have been acclaimed to-day by the whole world as the statesman whose brilliant and intuitive genius won the war. *Dis aliter visum,* and from First Lord of the Admiralty, with the formation of the first Coalition Government, he declined to the position of Chancellor of the Duchy of Lancaster.

His tenure of this minor office was not to be of long duration. He was given command of a Battalion in France, which he held for many months, and, indeed, until the unit was disbanded. When this happened, the Government and the Allied cause were alike sagging; and Churchill was advised by critics as acute as Lord Carson that his place was in the House of Commons. One story survives of his active service which is worth recording. When holding the Ploegsteert line the Battalion H.Q. occupied a very disagreeable farmhouse (I once had occasion to visit it) which from time to time was heavily shelled. A General on a round of inspection remonstrated with Winston, pointing out the danger of the position. Winston replied by making it plain that there was absolutely no other place available which would enable him to retain the necessary contact with his officers and men. The General did not attempt to make any suggestion, but repeated insistently and a little petulantly, "I tell you it is a very dangerous place." To whom Winston, most respectfully— "Yes, sir; but, after all, this is a very dangerous war."

Mr. Churchill, who at this time was being pursued by Mr. Gwynne of the *Morning Post* with the fussy, feeble rancour which that gentleman employs from time to time according to feminine orders, in the man-hunt of the moment, was not included in Mr. Lloyd George's Government at its formation. But an opportunity of adding to the Cabinet a mind so constructive and so suggestive was found when Dr. Addison left the Ministry of Munitions.

Here Winston was in his element, and the immense value of the public services he rendered, though well known to Sir Douglas Haig and his Staff, has never been sufficiently appreciated at home. The War Office still preserves a comparative chart illustrating the output of destructive agencies when he went to the Munitions Office and when he left it. Had he done no other work in the war he would have deserved well of the nation. His new office afforded unlimited scope alike for his ingenuity and his driving power. It may incidentally be observed that as First Lord of the Admiralty he had done more than any other individual to procure the adoption of the tank conception. I remember him describing to me its possibilities when I was on leave from France early in 1915. With his usual rhetorical brilliancy he depicted these great caterpillars marching over No Man's Land, eating up trenches, climbing hillocks, and jeering at every material obstacle. I thought he was mad; but, as I was his guest, I thought it polite to listen. I was, however, completely ignorant of the possibilities of mechanical locomotion of this kind. It was more serious that others who ought to have known better derided and disparaged the idea.

I still have a copy of a Cabinet paper in which Winston urged upon his colleagues the immense contribution to the war which machines of this kind might render. It was always his strong desire, when they were at last produced, that they should not be used until they were assembled in such numbers on the Western Front as to win a great, if not a decisive, victory. But the soldiers who had previously derided the invention—one sapient General describing it as "Winston's folly"—when once they were in possession of the tanks, could not wait. And accordingly the greatest mechanical invention which Great Britain or any other combatant Power contributed to land warfare was almost squandered by its employment in insufficient force. Safeguarded and multiplied, the tanks might yet have reproduced the victorious destructiveness of Hannibal's elephants.

It is of interest to note that in this matter at least contemporary justice was done to Churchill. The Committee which was appointed by Mr. Lloyd George's Government to report upon the credit and value of many different inventions made during the war measured in weighty language, which must have delighted him, the value and the force of his contribution to the discovery of tanks.

I do not propose to examine here Mr. Churchill's work since the Armistice. I was never able to share the sanguineness with which he surveyed each new attempt to dislodge the Soviet murderers. But, at least, his impulses were sound and his miscalculations—if they were miscalculations—will not, perhaps, be too severely censured at a moment when the whole world has so recently been shocked by the judicial murder of high ecclesiastical persons.

Of the man as he is known to his friends this is hardly the place to speak. He is generally supposed to be aggressive and truculent. He has many of the conversational powers of Dr. Johnson, and could be both if he wished. But no man living is more tolerant, more easy, more companionable, in social intercourse. And his charm and friendship are as well known as his genius. He is indeed *anima candidissima*. He is almost the only man whom I have ever known who simply could not speak, or acquiesce in, an untruth on a matter great or small, however convenient it might be.

Churchill fell with those of his colleagues who did not in a flash find salvation with Mr. Bonar Law. With his defeat at Dundee there passed for the moment from the Parliamentary scene a memorable, formidable, and vivid personality. He was, in my judgment, before he left it, the most powerful controversialist in the House of Commons. His form was literary and even classic; his arguments were lucidly conceived, logically arranged, and massively produced. In the Cabinet he was always an arresting, original, and eloquent adviser. It was not always necessary or perhaps wise to adopt his view, but no Cabinet could afford, and ours never did, to decide against him without giving the deepest consideration to the brilliant argument which rendered it so plausible.

An extreme section of the Conservative Party, to whom, paradoxically enough, he bears no small affinity, has definitely repelled him, with others, from the army which must hold the economic fort, upon which the commercial greatness of this country depends, from those who would subvert it. This is the fight—and this is the only fight—of the future.

With characteristic courage and independence he has chosen his side indifferent to the taunt that no man in English politics can change his party twice. Every fibre of his being is individualist; and in office or out of it—in Parliament or out of it—his sword will be flashing in the struggle which awaits us all. And as I survey the combative qualities of those who, equally with himself, are pledged to march in that crusade, I cannot think of one able to bring more decisive qualities to the issues which will so soon determine the genius of our people and the future of our civilisation.

LORD D'ABERNON: "A MIND OF GREAT FERTILITY" [23]

Lord D'Abernon was for six years after the war the British Ambassador in Berlin and a foremost advocate of reconciliation with the defeated Germans. This was also Churchill's theme.

[23] From Lord D'Abernon, *Portraits and Appreciations* (London, 1930), pp. 54-63. Reprinted by permission of Lord D'Abernon's executors. For Churchill's support of the policy of an Anglo-German rapprochement in the 1920s see also Lord D'Abernon, *An Ambassador Of Peace,* 3 volumes (London, 1929-31) .

What are the qualities or defects which make for notoriety? What are the virtues or vices which bring one individual so prominently into public notice and maintain him as a constant subject of discussion, whether in praise or blame? The characteristics required are unquestionably different from the attributes of greatness. Perhaps not incompatible though divergent. Advertisement, however sedulously pursued, is powerless to overcome the absence of original endowment, nor can it be said that fame always comes to those who most ardently pursue it.

These reflections rise naturally to the mind in considering the career of Winston Churchill, for no one in living recollection has attained notoriety—in the good sense—to an extent comparable with him. Exceptional as are his talents, brilliant as are his achievements, they would not account for the unique place which he holds in the attention of the public but for the possession by him of some gift withheld from others. This gift is usually described as an outstanding personality. Whether this expression adds much to our comprehension of the matter may be doubted. The fact remains that at any time during the last thirty years, ever since he entered public life, Winston has been the universal and inevitable subject of discussion in every kind of society. Even in those circles least favourable to him, least in sympathy with his ardent personal ambition, no general conversation lasted long without lapsing into Winstoniana. This fact obtained in mess-rooms, in golf clubs, and in the most philistine resorts, where in earlier years there was more criticism than approbation. Men and women are led by an obscure but irresistible instinct to discuss Winston.

In insisting upon his unique power of attracting the limelight, much as a lightning-conductor attracts lightning, there is some danger of underrating Winston's real ability. Nothing could be farther from my intention, for he is not only the best equipped political combatant of his generation, but has a facility in many directions which approaches genius. As a speaker and debater he is in the front rank; as a coiner of phrases unequalled among contemporaries; as a writer he is the rival if not the superior of the best professionals—in courage undaunted—in openness of mind an example to all.

His mental alertness is astonishing. Perhaps the most picturesque proof of this may be found in his artistic career. Without special interest in art or in the theory of æsthetics, he one day thought he would like to paint. Unhampered by arduous training or tuition, he seized paint-brushes and a palette, producing in a short time, without outside assistance or guidance, works of such merit that they were sold at fair prices in the open market in competition with the productions of professional men. Success was so marked that his further development in the direction of artistic achievement was awaited with some trepidation by the fashionable painters of the hour. Happily for them the attempt of well-meaning friends to guide his native genius into the beaten paths of academic correctness so damped his ardour that the artistic impetus petered out, his superfluous energy being later diverted to bricklaying. . . .

To say of a statesman that he possesses a lively intelligence is to suggest some lightness of mettle. It is impossible to deny liveliness to Winston, but the calibre of the guns he carries is certainly not light. Some of his initiatives may have gone west, notably those with which the public are best acquainted. The defence of Antwerp, the attack on the Dardanelles, injured his reputation for wisdom—injured it perhaps unduly. On the other hand, the bold decision to keep the British Fleet together in July 1914 won for him universal approbation. In my opinion, his attitude in each of these events, the successful and the unsuccessful alike, was indicative of a powerful mind, untrammelled by official routine, unaffrighted by personal responsibility.

With regard to Antwerp and the Dardanelles, it is by no means proved that the conception was wrong: half-hearted adoption by colleagues, delay in execution, may have married what was in itself sound strategy. It is worthy of note regarding Antwerp that von Kluck, judging after the event and with full knowledge of all the circumstances, has expressed his adherence to a strategic plan not dissimilar to that of Antwerp, viz. a plan in which the British Expeditionary Force would have been sent to Amiens threatening the flank of the German right in its advance on Paris, a conception broadly analogous to Winston's. In the case of the Dardanelles, all German authorities who have written on the subject are agreed that the British attack was within an ace of succeeding. Success would have caused panic in Constantinople, and would have driven the German Embassy from Pera into the wilds of Asia Minor.

Some critics have held that Churchill's real talent lies in literature and in rhetoric rather than in administration and statesmanship. It has been indicated that there are reasons for dissenting from the view that there is in him any absence of practical wisdom. Perhaps it is too soon to pass a final verdict. When the time comes for the publication of the very numerous memoranda which he submitted during the War to every Cabinet of which he was a member, judgment will be pronounced. No one has left on paper fuller material for condemnation or acquittal. While others talked, Winston both talked and wrote. This is clearly apparent from Asquith's Memoirs. A further impression is derived from them, namely that Winston had more ideas, more electrical force, and presented political memoranda in greater profusion than any other member of the Cabinet, while in strategic proposals he was hardly less prolific than the entire General Staff.

If a balance is to be struck between literary talent on one side and political ability on the other, the merit of both has to be estimated, and the literary merit of Churchill stands high. In the long course of British history it is doubtful if any Minister of the first rank, burdened as all Ministers must be by the cares of office, has made a contribution to history and literature superior to Churchill's. He stands the test, whether in volume, range, or quality. So unique a record reveals not only a mind of great fertility, but an extraordinary facility for keeping alive contemporaneously— without mutual injury—interests of various kinds.

It might be expected that such a man, driven forward by a teeming brain, tormented by grandiose conceptions struggling for expression and execution, would have the haggard appearance of the jaded worker, or would suffer in an exaggerated degree from the nervosity of the *genus irritabile vatum.*

Nothing of the kind; Winston is genial, affectionate, humorous— the best of friends, a generous opponent, taking criticism and enduring disappointment with a smile, half amused at his own career and half surprised at his astonishing success. Still boyish in mind and manner after twenty years of high office, retaining a faculty for the acquisition of knowledge which has not deserted him with increasing years. He might, indeed, without undue assumption, blazon on his escutcheon Goya's noble profession of faith, "Aun

aprendo" (I continue to learn) rather than the less appropriate
motto of the Churchills, "Fiel pero desdichado" (Faithful but unfortunate).

EMANUEL SHINWELL: LABOUR LOOKS AT CHURCHILL [24]

*Emanuel Shinwell, a Socialist of strong and sincere con-
victions, frequently crossed swords with Churchill in debate.
Yet he saw that his opponent and "enemy" was not the angry,
autocratic personality of Labour legend.*

Nobody in British politics during the early 'twenties inspired
more dislike in Labour circles than Winston Churchill. His crown-
ing sin was the fatuous declaration that Labour was unfit to govern,
an accusation that gave the gravest offence to members of the Labour
Party. "What right," it was asked, "had he to talk in this arrogant
fashion," thus disparaging responsible Labour leaders like Arthur
Henderson, George Barnes and J. R. Clynes, all members of the
Coalition Government, whose ability and industry had won the
respect of their Conservative and Liberal colleagues?

In those days criticism of Churchill was the outstanding feature
at meetings organised by the Labour Movement. In every market-
place Labour propagandists dwelt upon his eccentricities, quoted
his fulminations against the Conservative Party when he was a
Liberal and sought with impassioned oratory to expose the iniqui-
ties of this "wayward genius." Regarded as the principal impediment to Labour's progress, he became the target for almost every
epithet in the English language.

When I entered Parliament in 1922, Churchill was not a Member.
His sensational rejection by the electors of Dundee at the previous
Election was hailed with unconcealed delight by the Labour Party
throughout the country. This was the year in which a tremendous
political transformation caused the return of the largest number of

[24] From Emanuel Shinwell, "Churchill as a Political Opponent," in Charles
Eade, ed., *Churchill By His Contemporaries* (London, 1953), Chap. 9, pp. 75-83.
Reprinted by permission of the Rt. Hon. Emanuel Shinwell, Miss Diana Eade
and Charles Eade's executor. A post-1945 picture of Churchill from a Labour
Party politician (subsequently a Cabinet Minister in Harold Wilson's government) is to be found in R. H. S. Crossman, *The Charm of Politics* (London,
1958), in the form of a review of Churchill's first volume of war memoirs.

Labour Members of Parliament the House of Commons had ever known. Not less satisfactory was the defeat of Churchill, Labour's most dangerous opponent, and—there were few who would have dared to deny it—the most brilliant of them all. There were unprecedented scenes of enthusiasm at Election celebrations. Many thought that the day of revolution had arrived. "Give us another Election," they declared, "and we shall wipe both Conservative and Liberals out of existence."

The Election of 1924 failed to bear out the promise of 1922. It was, for many of us, a tragic event. I lost my seat and did not return to Parliament until early in 1928. Meanwhile, Churchill, who had successfully fought Epping, had joined the Baldwin Government. His activities as Chancellor of the Exchequer and as the self-appointed defender of the Constitution during the General Strike served to embitter relations still further between him and the Labour Movement. He was accused of taking decisions that led to a sharp increase in unemployment, of raiding State funds in the interests of wealthy taxpayers, and of rejecting attempts to compromise in the General Strike, thus prolonging the dispute. Nor was his conduct as Editor of the official anti-strike paper, the British Gazette, calculated to enhance his reputation among the industrial workers. The mention of his name at Labour gatherings was the signal for derisive cheers; when a Labour speaker found himself short of arguments, he only had to say "Down with Winston Churchill." This never failed to draw thunderous applause. Undoubtedly, he was our most valuable propaganda asset. . . .

During Labour's second term of office—this time as the largest single Party in the House of Commons—Churchill seldom restrained his feelings. Nobody on the Front Opposition Bench assailed the Government with greater violence. His frequent bouts with Philip Snowden, Labour's Chancellor of the Exchequer, were the highlights of our debates. But Snowden, with his penetrating logic and vitriolic tongue, proved more than a match for the scintillating orator of the Tory Opposition.

It was otherwise with Ramsay MacDonald: he detested Churchill: his dislike of an opponent increased in the measure of the criticism directed against him. Churchill never ceased to jibe and sneer at MacDonald. One memorable passage sticks in my memory. After a reference to MacDonald's skill in falling without hurting himself he recalled a visit when a child to a circus which contained an exhibition of freaks and monstrosities. "The exhibit he most desired to see was the 'Boneless Wonder.' His parents objected to his taste in wishing to see such a revolting spectacle so he had to wait fifty years to see the 'Boneless Wonder' sitting on the Treasury Bench." This cruel jibe created considerable amusement on the Opposition Benches but caused MacDonald's followers to vent all their spleen on Churchill. The junior members of the Government who were among MacDonald's ardent supporters, strained at the leash. They could not assail Churchill in the House—junior Ministers are only permitted to speak when instructed. They did, however, give full rein to their emotions in public about the man who was regarded as the Labour Party's most formidable opponent.

The economic crisis of 1931 brought further frustration. Our principal leaders, MacDonald and Snowden, had forsaken us and gone over to the enemy. Worse still, many of us lost our seats at the General Election when Conservatives and Liberals, with a few Labourists, combined against us. Once more we were thrust back into the wilderness.

I fully expected that Churchill would now become a member of the National Government. He had been the Labour Government's principal antagonist and had conspired to bring about its downfall. But while the ablest man in the Tory Party was placed on the shelf Baldwin appointed some of the stodgiest creatures that ever disgraced the Treasury Bench. No wonder Churchill regarded them with contempt.

Among his friends there was a general conviction that this was the twilight of his career, but the debates on the India Bill continued and some of Churchill's most powerful speeches were heard in Parliament—however unpalatable they were to those of us who rejected his imperialistic and reactionary opinions.

It was not until after the Election in 1935 that I made actual contact with Churchill. Once again I was on the Opposition Benches —this time as the Member for the Seaham Division. I had ousted my former Leader, MacDonald, in one of the most bitterly contested fights in the Election—and by a huge majority.

And then began that memorable series of speeches by Churchill where the case for rearmament was argued with a skill, lucidity and earnestness which, if it failed to convince the Labour benches, at least earned for the orator the admiration his qualities deserved. Among the Tories his advocacy of more adequate defence preparations, far from gaining unqualified support, created considerable confusion. Bitter exchanges ensued between Baldwin and his former Chancellor of the Exchequer, while on the benches immediately behind Churchill sat a group of Tories who persistently interjected, treating his remarks with derision. . . .

Churchill has often referred to differences in the Labour Party —no doubt with malicious intent. In turn, I have reminded him of his criticism of the Baldwin and Chamberlain Governments which angered all his colleagues, of the heated exchanges and of his long sojourn in the wilderness. It is no exaggeration to say that, while the Labour Party vehemently opposed him, they were more conscious of his gifts than many of those on his own side of the House. Here was this striking figure in our political life, this sparkling orator who had held the highest offices in the State, who presented his case with unquestionable sincerity, however misguided we regarded it—scorned by his former colleagues. One could, so it seemed to me, dispose quite easily of his arguments, yet his resolution, his marshalling of the facts and his industry, elevated him above his fellows, most of whom were political midgets in comparison.

How could Baldwin ignore Churchill's abilities in the sphere of defence by appointing Sir Thomas Inskip as the Minister for the Co-ordination of Defence, who yielded nothing but a weary collection of turgid utterances in our debates, and bored the House to such a degree that hardly anybody could be induced to stay and listen to him?

I must frankly admit that any admiration that I felt for Churchill seldom prevented me from indulging in sharp and no doubt irrelevant interjections, but these were inspired more by any anxiety to widen the cleavage in the Tory ranks than out of discourtesy. Often enough he gave me more than I had bargained for—but what of that? I was gaining experience in the Parliamentary cut-and-thrust of debate. Moreover it was his own technique. In Opposition, he maintained a constant stream of interjections, some audible and to the point, but often quite unintelligible.

What intrigued me above all else was the manner of his treatment by the Tory Members. I have watched him, accompanied by a sole companion, walking broodingly through the corridors of the House, or conversing in the smoke-room with a few admirers like Brendan Bracken and Robert Boothby. But generally, Tory members gave him a wide berth.

Then we came to those fateful days when many of his predictions, far from being falsified, were justified in the event.

HAROLD NICOLSON: "THE MOST INTERESTING MAN IN ENGLAND" [25]

Harold Nicolson was a National Labour Member of Parliament, a talented writer and historian, and not a man to suffer fools gladly. At a time when Churchill's political fortunes were at their lowest ebb, Nicolson focused on his abilities and prophesied his future.

Winston Churchill is the most interesting man in England. He is more than interesting; he is a phenomenon, an enigma. How can a man so versatile and so brilliant avoid being considered volatile and unsound? He will live in English history long after those who have made it are forgotten, for he is an Anglo-American freak, and England loves her freaks devotedly (once they are safely dead). Before he was twenty-six, he had seen more fighting than the oldest general. He was a Member of Parliament before he was twenty-seven, a Member of the Ministry before he was thirty-one, and a full-blown Cabinet Minister at thirty-four. Since then he has been Minister of Commerce, Colonies, Navy, Munitions, Home Affairs, War, Air and Treasury. He devised the Antwerp and the Dardanelles campaigns, and it was not his fault that they failed. He adopted the device of tanks for trench warfare, and it was not his fault that they were used too soon. It is largely to him that the Irish settlement is to be attributed. He is the best living writer of English narrative prose. He is a landscape painter and can do anything from playing polo to bricklaying. His dominant qualities

[25] From an article by Harold Nicolson published in *Vanity Fair*, 1931. Reprinted by permission of Sir Harold Nicolson. There are many fascinating references to Churchill's isolation and opinions during the 1930s in Harold Nicolson, *Diaries and Letters, 1930-39,* ed. Nigel Nicolson (London, 1966).

are imagination, courage and loyalty; his dominant defect, impatience.

He is a man who leads forlorn hopes, and when the hopes of England become forlorn, he will once again be summoned to leadership.

SIR ARTHUR SALTER: THE WILDERNESS YEARS [26]

Sir Arthur Salter was a public servant and administrator who played a leading part during both world wars in making sure that Britain's shipping lifeline was kept open, despite continual and severe German submarine attack. As he saw it, the wilderness years were a vital maturing period in Churchill's life.

It was in these years in the wilderness that Mr. Churchill began his greatest service to the country and brought his own qualities to their fullest maturity. If the biographer will turn, for his understanding of the Churchill of 1940, first to the few crowded years of youth between 1896 and 1900, he will perhaps next study, not his years of office, but what he did in the long intervening period. He was in fact, with unremitting industry and energy, doing two things. He was urging the necessity of stronger national and Empire defence with the authority of one who had held, and the freedom of one who no longer held, high office; and he was writing, and in doing so learning, history. In writing on the first World War he necessarily reflected on the conclusions to be drawn from it. The work he did in writing the life of his ancestor, the Duke of Marlborough, did even more. The roots of his intellectual life were henceforth deeper and stronger; he reached his full maturity. By becoming a historian he crowned and completed his equipment as a statesman. When he faced his greatest task he did so, as no other living man could have done—and as he himself could not have done earlier in life—as the embodiment of British history and tradition. He was the essential Englishman—the British 'Everyman,' in the sense of being what every man then wished to be.

[26] From Sir Arthur Salter, *Personality in Politics* (London, 1947), pp. 94-95. Reprinted by permission of the Rt. Hon. Lord Salter. Lord Salter's most recent volume, *Slave of the Lamp: A Public Servant's Notebook* (London, 1967), is also of value in understanding recent British politics.

VINCENT SHEEAN: A MIND TEMPERED FOR CRISIS [27]

*The American writer Vincent Sheean first met Churchill in
1935, when both men were on vacation in a villa on the
south of France. For three successive summers Sheean observed
Churchill closely. His shrewd analysis of Churchill's position
and views during these last three wilderness years gives an
accurate and vivid picture of a man, all of whose many enemies,
and some of whose friends, now considered him too old and
too anachronistic to play any further constructive role in politics or world affairs. Churchill was now over sixty.*

Mr. Churchill, in spite of the fact that he was on holiday,
painting and taking the sun, could not keep his mind off these
ominous foreshadows of the day of reckoning. He spoke constantly
of the Ethiopian crisis, of the League, of Mussolini, of relations
between England and Italy, of Italy's relations with Germany, and
of German rearmament. German rearmament afflicted him then
sorely, for he had just come upon some incontrovertible evidence
of the extent to which it was being pushed forward by the single-
minded Nazis. He had already spoken publicly, and was to speak
more than once in the coming years, of what this portended for
England. His words had been unheard. He had been out of power
since 1931—they had preferred Neville Chamberlain to him in
making up the new "National" cabinet—and was to remain in
the wilderness until adversity swept him in again. Most observers
thought him unlikely ever to regain a position of first rank in
English politics, for he had, to all intents and purposes, lost his
party. The Tories did not like or trust him; he was not "safe."
They said he was too "brilliant"—what is called "too clever." He
could not return to the Liberals, because his views on imperialism
were not theirs, and besides the Liberal party had almost passed
out of existence. He was conspicuous in the House of Commons
and in the country, but as a lone eccentric, too familiar for too long,
a character too blazingly and relentlessly famous for any further
use in the humdrum business of government. What England wanted
was good, substantial, mediocre men like Stanley Baldwin and

[27] From Vincent Sheean, *Between the Thunder and the Sun* (London, 1943),
pp. 41-42, 43-44 and 45-47. Reprinted by permission of Vincent Sheean.

Neville Chamberlain. The pipe of the earlier sage, like the umbrella of the later one, came to have symbolic value in English minds: it represented the solid, uneventful virtue of stupidity, the most popular quality in public life everywhere during periods when men feel comfortable and safe.

Winston was "out"—definitely, and, as it seemed, permanently, "out." Even so he could not divorce his interests from those of the nation. He was deeply concerned over the developing crisis and read everything he could find on it in English and French. From the outset he seemed to see that it was not merely a question of a colonial adventure in Ethiopia, but involved the whole structure of Europe, with possibilities of realignment carrying the promise of deadly danger to England. This sense of what was contained in the germ —was what most sharply distinguished Mr. Churchill's attitude toward these matters from the attitudes of the Baldwin-Chamberlain puddingheads who were in power through the 1930s. He could see past, present and future in relation; he knew how to watch, could feel them develop, was quick—even at his age—to develop with them. In the few years since I first heard him talk he has traversed a huge distance in political thought: in 1935 he would not speak to his old colleagues and friends if they had been in favour of even the most modest constitutional reform in India; and in 1942 he was offering India her freedom. . . .

He had a distinction which he tried to bring out in every talk about Ethiopia just then: it seemed to him very important. "It's not the thing we object to," he would say, "it's the *kind* of thing." I had not then succumbed as much to his genial charm as I did later, and I could not quite accept this. I mentioned the Red Sea, the route to India, the importance of Aden. Mr. Churchill brushed all that aside: "We don't need to worry about the Italians," he said. "It isn't that at all. It isn't the thing. It's the kind of thing."

The distinction was worth making, because hardly anybody in Europe could take England's high-minded ethical protests seriously just then. Obviously the British Empire had been created by precisely the kind of thing Mussolini was now about to attempt in Ethiopia—although, in an age of slower communication, it had grown up more naturally and less by deliberate plan. Mr. Churchill was pinned down firmly one day by an elegant lady, Mme. Letellier, who said that an objection to the thing might be practical and necessary, but that England had no historical right to object to the kind of thing. England had too often profited by "the kind of thing."

"Ah, but you see, all that belongs to the unregenerate past, is locked away in the limbo of the old, the wicked days," Mr. Churchill said, smiling benevolently upon her across the luncheon-table. "The world progresses. We have endeavoured, by means of the League of Nations and the whole fabric of international law, to make it impossible for nations nowadays to infringe upon each other's rights. In trying to upset the empire of Ethiopia, Mussolini is making a most dangerous and foolhardy attack upon the whole established structure, and the results of such an attack are quite incalculable. Who is to say what will come of it in a year, or two, or three? With Germany arming at breakneck speed, England lost in a pacifist dream, France corrupt and torn by dissension, America remote and indifferent—madame, my dear lady, do you not tremble for your children?" . . . He was a parliamentarian of parliamentarians, a true House of Commons man, a Liberal in the nineteenth-century sense, a Whig in an earlier sense. The institutions of representative constitutional government meant a great deal to him. They had so entwined themselves about his earliest memories and his lifelong preoccupations that he was sometimes only half conscious of the force with which they influenced his every developed thought. He showed by indirection, allusively and sometimes in the most unthinking assumptions, that he regarded representative democracy as not only the highest form of government, but as the only one under which mankind could evolve in relative freedom. His temperamental dislike for Nazi excesses, for all forms of tyranny, for cruelty, disorder and corrupt or summary courts of law, was the counterpart of this Whiggish insistence upon representative democracy as the only good form of rule. In some ways I should have expected him to be more favourable to the Fascist dictators than the other English political men; he was class-conscious, or had been, and had seemed to dread working-class revolution more than most people in the early 1920s. You might therefore have expected him to succumb to the Fascist argument that Fascism was a bulwark against Communism. I think at the outset he was rather favourable to Mussolini, whom he originally admired, but he was never taken in by the Fascist pretence of historical necessity. He was too intelligent and he knew too much history for that. On the contrary, when Hitler arose to put Mussolini's principles into more serious and dangerous practice, Mr. Churchill saw the trap immediately and reacted with his utmost vigour. His patriotism was rapidly engulfing all other sentiments, emotions and prejudices, so that the awareness of danger to England drove out whatever had originally prepared him for benevolence toward the Fascist principle, and he was willing, in the end, to work with the extreme Left if necessary to defeat the paramount enemy. This evolution I saw. I do not know if Mr. Churchill is aware that I saw it—at first he paid little attention to me—but from 1935 to 1939 were the precise years in which he was traversing this immense ideological area, and it was then (while he was out of office) that his mind was tempered for the supreme crisis. When I first talked to him about Spain he was pro-Franco and greatly concerned over Russian intervention; when I last talked to him (just before the fall of the Spanish Republic) he was saddened and made solemn by the whole thing, perceived the importance of the victory for Hitler and Mussolini, and regarded the fall of the Republic as a blow to England. Again, with respect to Russia, and most of all with respect to India, these few years produced in him such extraordinary process of ageing and tempering that he could hardly be recognised, in 1942, as the man who had once thumbed his nose gaily at the whole world outside the British Isles.

STANLEY BALDWIN: ELOQUENCE WITHOUT WISDOM [28]

The Prime Minister, Stanley Baldwin, persisted in disregarding Churchill's warnings about the need to strengthen Britain's defenses and to find allies to check the possible march of German power. He told his friend Thomas Jones in 1936:

One of these days I'll make a few casual remarks about Winston. Not a speech—no oratory—just a few words in passing. I've got it all ready. I am going to say that when Winston was born

[28] Quoted in Thomas Jones, *A Diary With Letters, 1931-1950* (London, 1954), p. 204. Reprinted by permission of the Oxford University Press. For a discussion of British policy toward Nazi Germany, and Churchill's opposition to it, see Martin Gilbert and Richard Gott, *The Appeasers* (Boston, 1963).

lots of fairies swooped down on his cradle gifts—imagination, eloquence, industry, ability, and then came a fairy who said "No one
person has a right to so many gifts" picked him up and gave him
such a shake and twist that with all these gifts he was denied judgment and wisdom. And that is why while we delight to listen to him
in this House we do not take his advice.

ADOLF HITLER: "CHURCHILL, FEEL YOURSELF HONOURED" [29]

*In November 1938 the German Chancellor, Adolf Hitler,
began to single out Churchill for sarcastic attack in his speeches
and derided Churchill's criticisms of the Nazi regime.*

The Governments of the Democratic countries are compelled
to maintain freedom, even if it leads to war-mongering. Churchill
said he was of the opinion that the German regime ought to be
destroyed with the co-operation of forces within Germany, who
would probably place themselves thankfully at his disposal. If
Churchill communicated less with emigrant circles, that is, with
traitors maintained and paid by foreign countries, and more with
Germans, he would then realise the folly and stupidity of his remarks.

I can assure this gentleman, who appears to live on the moon,
that such forces opposed to the regime do not exist in Germany.
There is only one force—the National Socialist movement and its
leadership and armed forces. I naturally cannot prevent the possibility of this gentleman entering the Government in a couple of
years, but I can assure you that I will prevent him from destroying
Germany. As long as people talk about disarmament and leave the
war-mongers to carry on, I assume that their desire is to steal our
weapons and to bring about again our fate of 1918. I can tell
Churchill that it happened only once and that it will not happen
again!

[29] Quoted in Charles Eade, ed., *Churchill By His Contemporaries* (London,
1953), pp. 138-39. Churchill's prewar opinion of Hitler will be found in *Great
Contemporaries* (London, 1937), pp. 261-69. Hitler's anger was no doubt pro-
voked by Churchill's powerful attack on the Munich Agreement, Nazism, and
appeasement, made on October 5, 1938, in the House of Commons. This speech
should be read in full in *Hansard*. It constitutes a comprehensive indictment of
British policy toward Hitler at this time (see also p. 54 of this volume).

If Churchill says, "I don't hate the Germans: they are only a danger to us!" I can only reply, "That is the same here." If there is any man in the world who is authorized to speak for Germany, then I am that man and no one else. After all, Churchill may have 14,000, 20,000 or 30,000 votes behind him—I am not so well informed about that—but I have 40,000,000 votes behind me. The German regime is entirely a matter for the German people, and I will never allow any such foreign schoolmasters or governesses to interfere with it. If these English solicitors of world democracy argue that in one year we have destroyed two democracies, I can only ask—Goodness gracious, after all, what is democracy? Who defines it? Has the Almighty perhaps handed the key to democracy to such people as Churchill? I am only the advocate of Germany. I am not like Churchill, and heaven knows what oppositionalists, who style themselves advocates of the world. If Churchill says, "How is it that the Head of a State can cross swords with a British parliamentarian?" I must say, "Churchill, feel yourself honoured. You may gauge from this how highly esteemed British parliamentarians are in Germany that even the Head of the State does not hesitate to cross swords with one."

LOUIS FISCHER: "THE TOTAL IMPRESSION IS POWER" [30]

When the war came in September 1939 Churchill entered the War Cabinet. In May 1940, when the war was going badly for Britain and France, he was called upon to be Prime Minister, and was supported by both the Conservative and Labour Parties. As Prime Minister of a Coalition Government he was above party politics. He declared that he had only one aim: victory. Shortly after he became Prime Minister, an American writer, Louis Fischer, visited him at 10 Downing Street and observed him closely. Churchill was now sixty-five.

We sat opposite one another at a small round table. He smoked a very fat cigar and dropped ashes on his vest and occasionally brushed them off with the back of his hand. Across his

[30] From Louis Fischer, *Men and Politics* (London, 1941), pp. 587-88. Reprinted by permission of Louis Fischer and his publishers, Jonathan Cape Limited of London and Duell, Sloan and Pearce of New York.

vest was a gold chain of big links. His eyes look watery and tired. His face is huge and flabby and the lips have a fleshy droop. Yet the total impression is power. The upper half of his face is intellect, the lower half British bulldog. He speaks with a slight impediment, and his s's have a suspicion of s-h. He let me stay for thirty minutes. I talked much in the first five minutes and the rest of the time he replied to my brief questions. I enjoyed his English. He rolls out an ordinary sentence with the rounded finish and force of a carefully polished work of art. Churchill's English has the simple power of the language of the Bible. His nouns are pictures and his verbs work.

I think his strength lies in the fact that he doubts and does not doubt. He is coldly critical of his own country's weaknesses and mistakes. Enthusiasm does not blunt analysis; hopes do not distort facts. He thinks while he fights. He dares to have thoughts and doubts about conditions because he has no doubts about his course of action. He knows what he wants to do. There is no way back. There is only the struggle. The civilized brain in the upper storey does not hamper the animal determination in the lower storey.

Neville Chamberlain could not be a good war leader because he had prepared his mind for peace. But ever since the advent of Hitler in 1933, Winston Churchill had prepared his mind, and had wished to prepare his country, for war. When war came Churchill was brought into the government. Soon Churchill headed the government and spoke for England. He is England. The Englishman is narrowly insular, yet made broadly international by the Empire and trade. He is rooted deep in the old rock of the isle but he reacts to changes in the world's weather. For every Conservative Briton who looks backward there are at least three who see national survival in terms of progress and adaptation. In social legislation and civil liberties, Great Britain was always far in advance of any other great power. Churchill, I could see, is a fervid devotee of freedom. It is not merely a war motto or a war aim, but a component part of his life fibre. Of course, there is India. That is a serious blemish. But whose mentality has no blind spots? Like Lloyd George, Churchill is capable of indignation, passion, hard work, and bluntness. He convinces others not so much with words as by the contagiously axiomatic nature of his own convictions. "There will always be an England" is very Churchillian—and very British.

VISCOUNT MONTGOMERY: "HE MUST DOMINATE" [31]

During wars generals are always thought to be frightened of politicians, and politicians to be jealous of generals. General Montgomery, who became a Field-Marshal in 1944, commanded the British Eighth Army in North Africa, and was made Commander-in-Chief of the Allied Armies in Northern France after the Normandy landings. He later wrote a brief but revealing account of his relationship with the Prime Minister.

We did not always see eye to eye; I doubt if any soldier ever has done with his political chief, and certainly not with that one. But we did not have in the Second World War the rows that developed between soldiers and politicians in the First; that was due to Churchill. It was also due to the fact that we had in existence the British Chiefs of Staff Committee, a constitutional body responsible direct to, and effectively tied-in with, the War Cabinet. In the 1914-1918 War we had no such body and one has only to read Lord Beaverbrook's book MEN AND POWER to learn of the appalling rows and intrigues which went out between the "Frocks" and the "Brass-hats" in those days.

Whatever may have been his private views, I personally know of no case in which Churchill insisted on his own ideas being carried out once he was opposed by the united British Chiefs of Staff—provided they stood firm and did not retreat when bullied. And they did not retreat.

It has always seemed to me that Winston Churchill combined within himself—within one man—almost all the qualities which we humans can possess, and, as with all humans, they were not by any means all good. Of all his remarkable traits I would put "Domination" as the most prominent. He must dominate. He certainly dominated the events and persons surrounding him in the war years, as should all good leaders; you could look out for squalls if he was prevented from doing so. As time went on I ceased to regard him as my political chief. He became my friend. We were "Winston" and "Monty," and so it is today and will be ever after.

<hr>

[31] From Montgomery of Alamein, *Memoirs* (London, 1958), pp. 535-36. Reprinted by permission of Field-Marshal Viscount Montgomery.

ANEURIN BEVAN: KEEPING CHURCHILL IN CHECK [32]

Often during the war, criticism of Churchill was voiced vigorously in Parliament. In July 1942 Aneurin Bevan, the leading Socialist orator of his day, supported the "Churchill Must Go" movement with an outspoken attack on the Prime Minister's leadership in the House of Commons.

It seems to me that there are three things wrong. First, the main strategy of the war has been wrong; second, the wrong weapons have been produced; and third, those weapons are being managed by men who are not trained in the use of them and who have not studied the use of modern weapons.

Why is the strategy wrong? I say, first, that it is because the Prime Minister, although possessing many other qualities, sometimes conceives of the war, it seems to me, in medieval terms, because he talks of it as if it was a tourney. But the strategy is wrong because the Prime Minister has a wrong instrument of Government. . . .

The Prime Minister has qualities of greatness—everybody knows that—but the trouble is that he has too much to do. He has not around him colleagues to whom he can delegate any of this matter concerning the central direction of the war. The result is that all these defects which he possesses are made dangerous, because the Prime Minister, among all his other qualities, has a gift of expression which is exceedingly dangerous. He very often mistakes verbal felicities for verbal inspiration. The Prime Minister will, in the course of an evening, produce a whole series of brilliant improvisations, but has not the machinery to carry them through. . . .

I seriously suggest to the House that whatever they may do about this motion, they should for Heaven's sake insist, at this grave hour, that the Prime Minister be kept under the charge of strong men who have no Departmental interest. . . .

[32] From *Hansard*, July 2, 1942. Reprinted by permission of the Controller of Her Majesty's Stationery Office. The debate, which was a vigorous one, should be read in full. It is a rare example, even in democratic countries, of unfettered criticism in wartime.

ALAN HERBERT: "SENSITIVE AS WELL AS TOUGH" [33]

Among Churchill's defenders during the "Churchill Must Go" campaign was the humorist Alan Herbert, then an independent Member of Parliament. He spoke up boldly for Churchill during the debate. He also watched Churchill closely while he was under attack.

At the end of the two unhappy, snappy, yet dignified days Mr. Churchill rose to reply. I know no other face in public life which so faithfully reflects so many moods. If I think of Stanley Baldwin or Neville Chamberlain, I see the same face always— though, Heaven knows, I saw them in every sort of scene of every sort of drama, including Munich and the Abdication. But the Churchill face—if I may say so without offence—has the range, the variety, of one of those indiarubber faces we used to play with in our youth. You pressed them, this way or that, and they looked all sorts of things, in turn. Mr. Churchill, being more of an artist than those other two, I suppose, is sensitive as well as tough: and the pressure of events and people adjusts and changes the face amazingly. There is that glorious happy beam, when it is the face of the sun or the face of a laughing baby, a rosy dimpled face; there is the face of the imp, the face of Puck in action, not so happy but alert and vital. There is the face of the Statesman, calm but brooding, a curtain drawn before tremendous things. There is the pugnacious damn-you-all face, with the chin well out, the face of 'blood and sweat and toil and tears.' There is the rather bored face in the Smoking Room, which makes the young Member think 'What the Hell shall I say? Or would it be better to say nothing?' Then—lest I should be thought to suggest bad manners, which I certainly do not intend—there is the sudden smile, and twinkle, which make the young man glad to be alive, and doubly glad that he was elected; for here he is, a mortal, on intimate terms with a god, in good humour. I have no doubt there are many other faces: and someone who knows about faces should study and describe them all. But,

[33] From A. P. Herbert, *Independent Member* (London, 1950), pp. 236-37. Reprinted by permission of Sir Alan Herbert. Herbert's speech during the July 2, 1942, debate is a fine one, and can be read in *Hansard,* or in his book from which this quotation is taken.

last, there is what I think of as the grey face of the black times—
times made black not by foreign enemies but by his own people,
times when, still defiant and full of faith, he deeply felt the stabs
of injustice or disloyalty or lack of understanding. I cannot describe
it, I hope I shall never see it again: but the whole face changed,
almost collapsed—you would not have said, if you did not know,
that it was the same assembly of flesh and blood and bone as the
beaming, shining, grown-up-baby-face we all have seen and loved.
How often I have peeped along the benches over the noses of
twenty Members and seen that face, and it has wrung my heart—
the bowed head, the scowl, the lips and chin thrust out, the eyes
aimed angrily below the Table—as it might be a great bull baited
by cunning little men.

H. G. WELLS: TIME TO RETIRE [34]

*Argument over Churchill's war policy continued with
growing fierceness from 1942 to the end of the war. As in
World War I, he was at times misrepresented as being nothing
but a man of war. It was forgotten that, just as he had the
capacity to wage war vigorously during wartime, so also he
had acted in the past as a conserver of peace and as a preacher
of reconciliation between former enemies. In 1944 H. G. Wells,
whose anti-Churchill views of 1920 we have already read (see
pages 106-7), returned to the attack.*

Winston Churchill, the present would-be British Führer, is a
person with a range of ideas limited to the adventures and opportunities of British political life. He has never given evidence of
thinking extensively or of any scientific or literary capacity. Now
he seems to have lost his head completely.

When the British people were blistered with humiliation by the
currish policy of the old Conservative gang in power, the pugnacity
of Winston brought him to the fore. The country liked fighting
and he delighted in fighting. For want of a better reason he became
the symbol of our national will for conflict, a role he has now out-
lived. . . .

His ideology, picked up in the garrison life of India, on the reefs

[34] Reprinted by permission of *Tribune*.

of South Africa, the national home, and the conversation of wealthy Conservative households, is a pitiful jumble of incoherent nonsense. A Boy Scout is better equipped. He has served his purpose and it is high time he retired upon his laurels before we forget the debt we owe him.

LESLIE HORE-BELISHA: "HE MEANT BUSINESS" [35]

In 1945 the Conservatives were rejected by the British electorate. Churchill, who had become leader of the Conservative Party during the war, fell with them as a Labour Government came into power. When Churchill returned as Prime Minister in 1951 after the Conservative electoral victory, he was a man of seventy-seven in poor health. He delegated most of the business of government to others. One of his wartime critics, Leslie Hore-Belisha, a former War Minister under Neville Chamberlain, observed him at this time, and wrote an appreciation of his methods. Although this is the analysis of a contemporary, it has many elements also of historical perspective. It gives a convincing picture of Churchill's enormous capacity for work, which kept him so well informed, and which made him so effective whether in opposition or in office.

What is the secret of Sir Winston Churchill's remarkable ability to impress, persuade and dominate, in his speeches, in conversation, in committee, in the Cabinet itself?

Firstly, I think, one must recognise that Churchill naturally and without apparent effort, looks and behaves like somebody important. He is "news" and looks news.

Throughout his political career, whether in Opposition or in Government, he has always been in the forefront. In appearance, in manner, in dress and, above all, in speech, he is an individualist.

He gets the last ounce out of the English language—his unique command of which is one of his most persuasive gifts—by his characteristic modulations of voice and by his defiantly Anglo-Saxon

[35] From Lord Hore-Belisha, "How Churchill Influences and Persuades," in Charles Eade, ed., *Churchill By His Contemporaries* (London, 1953). Chap. 30, pp. 269-76. Reprinted by permission of Miss Diana Eade and Charles Eade's Executor. Also of interest for its references to Churchill is R. J. Minney, ed., *The Private Papers of Leslie Hore-Belisha* (London, 1960).

pronunciation of foreign words. When he spoke of the "Narzis," for instance, the very lengthening of the vowel carried with it his message of contempt. By these means he can, when he wishes, make not only every phrase but every word significant.

His unusual hats which startled the public fancy in his early years have given place to the cigar, an equally precious gift to the cartoonist. Perhaps such foibles call attention to himself. But what of his V-sign? There we have his knack of evoking a patriotic emotion. It is a gesture of genius.

But all that is spectacular, showing that Churchill, almost alone among British political men, appreciates that an appeal can be addressed to the eye as well as to the ear.

More fundamental is his meticulous study of any subject under discussion. With care and patience he builds up a case. First he reads every document to be found on the subject, and with Churchill to read is to remember. Few men have a greater capacity for assimilating facts. I have never known him to go into a conference with an ill-prepared or half-digested case. He knows when he enters a Cabinet or Committee meeting what he wants done. He has a scheme, a plan, a solution. Not for him the patient hearing while others sort out their views. He takes the initiative with a proposal of his own for others to support or, if they are so inclined, attack. Many eminent statesmen, after listening to all sides of a case and carefully weighing the pros and cons, only then, and in a judicial manner, decide on a course of action. Balfour and Asquith were in this category.

But one would have an entirely wrong impression of Churchill if one visualised him only as a student of briefs and books and a protagonist of theoretical opinions. He is a man, par excellence, who believes in seeing for himself, and he has never lost that boyish characteristic of asking "how it works." He enjoined on me in my own Ministerial career not merely to accept advice but: "Always see for yourself. Once you have seen a thing working, you know how it works."

Throughout his life he has followed this "See for yourself" practice. As a young soldier he went off to Cuba because, at that time, it was the only place in the world where there was real fighting. As Home Secretary he startled his political associates by going almost into the firing line in the "Battle of Sidney Street." His top hat glistened among the policemen's helmets. As Prime Minister in war he took every opportunity of visiting the battlefronts, the munition factories, the airfields, the bomb-ruined houses of the people. It was all part of his method of getting to know the facts at first hand. Even the wall he built himself at Chartwell is a reflection of that part of his plan of life.

For the same reason he likes having models made of things that specially interest him. During the early part of the war he had an idea for a machine for tunnelling underground to burrow beneath enemy fortifications. So he had a model made, and having studied its possibilities he asked me to go to the Admiralty and see it. His aim was to break the stalemate of position warfare, just as he had hoped to do in the First World War with the tank.

He always has a fresh and original approach to an old problem, often by introducing some new device or gadget. On this plane are his siren suit and his shoes which do up with zip fasteners instead of laces. I remember an occasion when I had lost a most important bunch of keys. Churchill heard about it and told me that he had once had the same misfortune. But, he added, it could never happen again, so far as he was concerned, because he kept his keys on the ends of a thick, silver, snake-like chain. This chain, he explained went round his back, threaded through the sides of his braces and the bunches of keys at either end rested safely in his trouser pockets. They could not be lost. After telling me all this he went one better and had a similar chain made for me, which I still have. I have not lost my keys since!

Graphs and maps likewise appeal to his visual imagination and they are often included in his armoury when he is presenting a case. It was when he was a critic of the Government during the late 1930s that I first learned of his interest in such things. He was advocating the use of the rocket in anti-aircraft warfare and he showed me diagrams to illustrate its ballistic characteristics. On the wall of my room at the War Office was a map of Europe, which impressed him. He liked to stand with his hands on his hips looking at it and discussing the problems of the future. I gave him this map and he hung it in his study at Chartwell. . . .

He has a peculiar sensitivity of what is happening in the world and little escapes him. He does not wait until breakfast to read the morning papers, but often sends for them during the night when they come off the Press. I have a vivid recollection of seeing him frequently in the Smoking Room in the House of Commons absorbed in the early editions of the evening newspapers. Only when he has finished reading them is he prepared to talk.

In his power to influence and persuade Churchill has another great asset—his dogged determination. If he cannot win his way in an argument he will probably propose the adjournment of the meeting to another day, when he will appear again, reinforced with new and weightier evidence, facts and information, and renew the attack. He never gives up and he never accepts a negative for an answer. How many Prime Ministers have felt themselves strong enough to call upon the House of Commons formally to reverse a vote deliberately given? Yet Churchill did this in the war on the issue of Equal Pay for Equal Work for male and female school-teachers during the passage of the Education Bill.

Consider how he has risen superior to electoral defeats. When I was first elected to the House of Commons in 1923 Churchill was not a Member. He had been defeated at Dundee. He stood again at Leicester West and was defeated. He then tried at the Abbey Division of Westminster and again the electors rejected him. Three defeats in a row would have been enough for most men, but Churchill was not discouraged. He presented himself to the people of the Epping Division of Essex, where, although the constituency is now called Woodford, he has remained ever since.

Never does he envisage failure. I recall Dame Margaret Lloyd George telling me how Churchill had bought a farm. He was quite new then to farming.

"He insisted," Dame Margaret said, "that he was 'going to make it pay whatever it costs.'"

The farm would be something of a recreation but it would also be a study and a new interest; something from which he could learn as he always does from his hobbies, whether painting, bricklaying, making an ornamental garden, or, in more recent years, horse racing.

In an analysis of the sources of his power and influence it would be impossible to overestimate his tremendous capacity for work, which is enhanced by his equally tremendous capacity for relaxation. With him this takes the form not of idleness but of a change of occupation. While his brain is at work, I have often noticed he has a singular facility of resting his body. He will, for instance, do much of his reading and writing propped up in bed.

Churchill is a tough opponent. He is conscious of his strength, too, and is not reluctant to let his adversary of the moment realise his confidence. I remember once being engaged in a controversy with him and he had hit me pretty hard. Then in conversation he said, "If you attack me I shall strike back and, remember, while you have a 3.7-inch gun I have a 12-inch gun." This was a reference to the fact that he was Prime Minister, with all the authority of his position, whereas I was a critic. He gave his warning with a twinkle in his eye but I knew that he meant business. I nevertheless went into action, but it was not long before his high explosives and shrapnel were falling all around me. . . .

Those who have been close to Churchill know of his intense loyalty to friends, even if he falls out with them politically. While you are a friend you can expect support to the hilt. But you must know that if you cross him Churchill will be an unrelenting opponent. Yet even in the heat of the argument he will often retain a deep regard and even personal affection for the man he is fighting, particularly if the man he is fighting really fights back.

PART THREE

CHURCHILL IN RETROSPECT

*There can be no doubt of the massive, oaken stature
that history will accord to him.*
—PRIME MINISTER HAROLD WILSON

*The record of his triumphant passage will inspire free
hearts all over the globe.*
—PRESIDENT JOHN F. KENNEDY

The man *whose wide-ranging views we have tried
to portray here and whose contemporaries have, as we saw,
been so divided about him, can expect now that he is dead
to become the center of a prolonged and heated historical
controversy. His son Randolph is publishing the documents
by which he can be judged; others will then pick these bones
until they are dry. Here, so soon after his death, we can only
give a glimpse of what is to come, when the cheap sneers of
biased critics and the blind devotion of true and false friends
will both give way to a calm appraisal. A generation must pass
before the average Englishman, even if he is an academic historian, will be able to talk about Churchill without distortion.*

*The following seven extracts are far from impartial, but
they do give a retrospective picture. They attempt to assess
his life's work, and they are written without malice. Two,
though prompted by his death, try nevertheless to take a wide
and balanced view. The others are equally honest. Lady Asquith, his lifelong friend, writes perceptively of his strength
and weaknesses. Isaiah Berlin, the philosopher, compares him
with President Franklin D. Roosevelt. Leopold Amery, a former Cabinet colleague, contrasts him with Lloyd George. Sir
Arthur Bryant, the historian, discusses his war leadership. President John F. Kennedy, on the occasion of Churchill's becoming
an honorary citizen of the United States, summarizes briefly
but acutely the nature of his genius. Finally, two Labour men,
Prime Minister Harold Wilson and a leader writer of the
New Statesman, give, at the moment of Churchill's death,*

appraisals of his achievements which are striking, coming as they do from a political party which seldom supported Churchill's objectives, and which was always suspicious of his methods and intentions.

Lady Violet Bonham-Carter: "Defiant Snooks at All Authority"[1]

I cannot attempt to analyse, still less to transmit, the light of genius. But I will try to set down, as I remember them, some of the differences which struck me at the time between him and all the others, young and old, whom I had known.

First and foremost he was incalculable. He ran true to no form. There lurked in every thought and word the ambush of the unexpected. I felt also that the impact of life, ideas and even words upon his mind was not only vivid and immediate, but direct. Between him and them there was no shock-absorber of vicarious thought or precedent gleaned either from books or other minds. His relationship with all experience was first-hand.

My father and his friends were mostly scholars, steeped in the classical tradition, deeply imbued with academic knowledge, erudition and experience. Their intellectual granaries held the harvests of the past. On many themes they knew most of the arguments and all the answers to them. In certain fields of thought there was to them nothing new under the sun. But to Winston Churchill everything under the sun was new—seen and appraised as on the first day of creation. His approach to life was full of ardour and surprise. Even the eternal verities appeared to him to be an exciting personal discovery. (He often seemed annoyed to find that some of them had occurred to other people long ago.) And because they were so new to him he made them shine for me with a new meaning. However familiar his conclusion it had not been reached by any beaten track. His mind had found its own way everywhere.

[1] From Violet Bonham-Carter, *Winston Churchill as I Knew Him* (London and New York, 1965), pp. 17-18, 19-20, and 21. Reprinted by permission of Lady Asquith of Yarnbury and her publishers, Harcourt, Brace and World, Inc.

Again—unlike the scholars—he was intellectually quite uninhibited and unselfconscious. Nothing to him was trite. The whole world of thought was virgin soil. He did not seem to be the least ashamed of uttering truths so simple and eternal that on an other's lips they would be truisms. This was a precious gift he never lost. Nor was he afraid of using splendid language. Even as I listened flowing and vibrating to his words, I knew that many of my captious and astringent friends would label them as "bombast"—"rhetoric"—"heroics." But I also knew with certainty that if they did they would be wrong. There was nothing false, inflated, artificial in his eloquence. It was his natural idiom. His world was built and fashioned in heroic lines. He spoke its language.

One other, paradoxical, impression I carried away from this, our first encounter. Although he had the ageless quality of greatness I felt that he was curiously young. In fact, in some pedestrian ways, he made me feel that I was older. I felt that, although armed to the teeth for life's encounter, he was also strangely vulnerable, that he would need protection from, interpretation to, a humdrum world which would not easily apprehend or understand his genius. And in this last fear I was right. . . .

The attitude of the general public towards him at the time was, at best, one of expectant interest, curiosity and tolerant amusement, at worst one of mistrust and acid reprobation. In Tory and social circles he had for some years past been a red rag which turned the mildest cows into infuriated bulls. He was an outsider, a pusher, thruster and self-advertiser. After he crossed the Floor he became, in addition, a rat, a turncoat, an arriviste and, worst crime of all, one who had certainly arrived. To take him down a peg or even several pegs was not only a pleasure but a duty—to society and to the nation.

The Liberals were naturally far more discerning. To their credit they have never regarded intellect as a dangerous factor in a politician. They recognized his quality and they gloried in their glittering catch. But even among Liberals there were certain reservations and suspicions. He was "sound" on Free Trade, on South Africa and on Retrenchment, but what about Reform—and Peace? He appeared to have found fighting a rather too congenial occupation in the past. Had he got Liberalism in his bones? Would he stay put?

In private life, though he inspired devotion in his friends, he did not exercise on his contemporaries the fascination of his father Lord Randolph Churchill. I remember asking my father, who as a young man in his early days in Parliament had known and loved Lord Randolph, which of the two he rated higher, and his reply: "You can't compare them. Randolph was irresistible. He had incomparably more charm, more wit. But—Winston is by far the better fellow of the two."

It is true, I think, that though Winston Churchill impressed and often dazzled, he did not charm, or try to charm. He was as impervious to atmosphere as a diver in his bell. By a blessed fluke I found my way into the bell and never lost it. To me it was a far more exciting place than the watery elements it excluded. But for those outside it often seemed to be an impenetrable shell. He sometimes made a brilliant sortie—but in conversation he exhaled rather than inhaled, and this was occasionally and not unnaturally, resented by his interlocutors. I remember my stepmother, who enjoyed self-expression and indulged it to the full, complaining that he had "a noisy mind." . . .

Ordinary men and women were equally bewildered by his congenital incapacity to be commonplace. The British people like seeing in their statesmen a reflection of themselves, perhaps in slightly sublimated form. Lord Baldwin recognized this taste and assuaged it to the full. He realized that the public love to hear the tunes they know, and he played them with a masterly dexterity and skill.

I remember the Duke of Devonshire of that day, who suffered from deafness, once saying to my father of Lord Spencer: "I always hear him because I know exactly what he is going to say." The trouble with Winston Churchill was that no one ever knew what he was going to say—or do. The unpredictable is rarely popular. More often than not it is mistaken for the unreliable. The public like getting what they expect. They resent surprises and prefer being lulled to being startled. . . . As I got to know our rank and file I often wondered how these earnest, high-thinking and low-living men made head or tail of Winston, and still more what he made of them. There is no doubt that his political performance left them dazzled—and blinking, sometimes with a vague mistrust. Turning away from the sun they saw spots. I think that to them he seemed a Bird of Paradise, of brilliant plumage and incalculable habits.

To him they were impersonal units of that indispensable collective entity, a reliable majority. I could not conceive communication between him and them in any code but that of politics. They spoke, felt, thought and lived in such a different idiom from his own. Knowing both languages I realized that though they must become his workmates they could never be his playmates. I remember once telling him as I left the House of Commons that I must hurry home because we had a dinner party of forty that night. "Forty to dinner? And who are they?" "Oh—some of our Liberal members—Horridges and Berridges and Runcimen and Mastermen and Hornimen. . . ." He was vicariously aghast at the prospect. "My poor child—you call that a dinner-party? And what will happen to you in this grim galère?" He was amazed when I said I should enjoy it, and muttered something about "great causes to whose altar even gleaming youth must bring its sacrifice."

But to do him justice, he indulged in very little "play" even when it was offered in a more congruous and congenial context. He was entirely absorbed in his work and thought of little else. In spite of Tory rancour at his "treachery to his class" (and its reward) he was socially besieged, assailed and pursued by importunate hostesses. Like him or loathe him, no one could deny his reclame. He was the most discussed, conspicuous and contentious figure of his day inside the Government or out of it.

But pleasure might beckon, and the Sirens sing in vain, they could not coax his nose from the grindstone. Even at week-end parties where I sometimes met him he arrived accompanied by his work and often spent the whole morning toiling at it in his bedroom, appearing at luncheon still in its grip. On such occasions I watched with some amusement the heroic efforts of his female neighbours to derail his train of thought, and their discomfiture. His mind contained no insulating dodges or devices, no fireproof curtains or watertight compartments. Once engaged by a theme it was wholly possessed.

Action or speech transformed him. The clay became a mobile and translucent mask through which his inner being shone, transfusing it with light and fire. It then assumed an infinite variety of Protean shapes—in turn that of an orator, a pugilist, a statesman, or a Puckish schoolboy cocking defiant snooks at all authority. Every emotion was faithfully reflected. His was a face that could not keep a secret. His personality thrust its way through so forcibly that his features seemed irrelevant trappings of his intrinsic self. . . .

At balls as elsewhere he was impervious to his surroundings, blind and deaf to the gyrating couples, the band, the jostling, sparkling throng. I remember once in a momentary lull directing his attention to the appearance of a friend of his who crossed our line of vision looking her very best. "Look—there goes X. Isn't she looking lovely tonight?" He looked at her, appraised her beauty and replied, "Yes —there goes X—a great woman—sagacious—chaste." This choice of epithets took my breath away. There were a hundred different adjectives which could with truth have been applied to X. But if one had scoured the dictionary with a tooth-comb it would have been impossible to discover three which less described her. She was neither "sagacious," "chaste" nor "great." Did he, I wondered, know any more about the human content of these people who belonged to his own world than about that of the Liberal rank and file?

Yet about the greatest figures in the political field his estimates and judgments were curiously sound. He often gave me in those early days appraisals of his front-rank colleagues and opponents as penetrating and true as those recorded in much later years in his portrait gallery Great Contemporaries. I think that for him human beings fell, roughly, into three categories: the great figures whom he weighed, measured and assessed in a historical perspective and about whom his judgment rarely erred: the (so-called) average man and woman who often made no impact on his attention, let alone his mind; and lastly his friends—those who had found their way into his heart.

His friendship was a stronghold against which the gates of Hell could not prevail. There was an absolute quality in his loyalty, known only to those safe within its walls. Their battle was his own. He would concede no inch of ground, no smallest point against them. In a friend he would defend the indefensible, explain away the inexplicable, even forgive the unforgivable.

When Churchill died Lady Violet Bonham-Carter, who had been created Baroness Asquith of Yarnbury, made her maiden speech in the House of Lords, during the course of which she said:

I have heard him called "erratic," "unreliable," "not a safe man." Not safe enough to fill the armchair of a humdrum office in safe days, but when all was at stake, when our own survival and the fate of civilisation were rushing towards the rapids, then we saw him as the one man strong enough to save.

He could be Puck or prophet, sage or wit, above the battle, in the scrum, an epic poet or a tease. . . . And how he brought not only fortitude but gaiety to our grimmest hours! "We are expecting the coming invasion. So are the fishes!": thus he broadcast to the French people from a basement during the crashes of an air raid. Hearing his chuckle, we ignored the bombs and laughed with him.[2]

[2] From *Hansard*, January 25, 1964. Reprinted by permission of the Controller of Her Majesty's Stationery Office. This, and the other speeches made that same day, should be read in full.

Isaiah Berlin: Churchill and Roosevelt[3]

The philosopher and historian Isaiah Berlin reviewed the first volume of Churchill's war memoirs:

Writing of Dunkirk he says: 'Had I at this juncture faltered at all in the leading of the nation, I should have been hurled out of office. I was sure that every Minister was ready to be killed quite soon, and have all his family and possessions destroyed, rather than give in. In this they represented the House of Commons and almost all the people. It fell to me in these coming days and months to express their sentiments on suitable occasions. This I was able to do because they were mine also. There was a white glow, overpowering, sublime, which ran through our island from end to end.' And on the twenty-eighth of June of that year he told Lord Lothian, then ambassador in Washington, 'Your mood should be bland and phlegmatic. No one is downhearted here.'

These splendid sentences hardly do justice to his own part in creating the feeling which he describes. For Mr. Churchill is not a sensitive lens which absorbs and concentrates and reflects and amplifies the sentiments of others; unlike the European dictators, he does not play on public opinion like an instrument. In 1940 he assumed an indomitable stoutness, an unsurrendering quality on the part of his people, and carried on. If he did not represent the quintessence and epitome of what some, at any rate, of his fellow citizens feared and hoped in their hour of danger, this was because he idealised them with such intensity that in the end they approached his ideal and began to see themselves as he saw them: 'the buoyant and imperturbable temper of Britain which I had the honour to express'—

[3] From Isaiah Berlin, *Mr. Churchill in 1940* (London and New York, 1964) pp. 26-27, 36-39. Reprinted by permission of Sir Isaiah Berlin and of his publishers, John Murray and Houghton Mifflin Company.

it was indeed, but he had a lion's share in creating it. So hypnotic was the force of his words, so strong his faith, that by the sheer intensity of his eloquence he bound his spell upon them until it seemed to them that he was indeed speaking what was in their hearts and minds. Doubtless it was there; but largely dormant until he had awoken it within them.

After he had spoken to them in the summer of 1940 as no one has ever before or since, they conceived a new idea of themselves which their own prowess and the admiration of the world has since established as a heroic image in the history of mankind, like Thermopylae or the defeat of the Spanish Armada. They went forward into battle transformed by his words. The spirit which they found within them he had created within himself from his inner resources, and poured it into his nation, and took their vivid reaction for an original impulse on their part, which he merely had the honour to clothe in suitable words. He created a heroic mood and turned the fortunes of the Battle of Britain not by catching the mood of his surroundings (which was not indeed, at any time, one of craven panic or bewilderment or apathy, but somewhat confused; stouthearted but unorganised) but by being stubbornly impervious to it, as he has been to so many of the passing shades and tones of which the life around him has been composed.

Mr. Roosevelt was intrigued by the Russian Sphinx; Mr. Churchill instinctively recoiled from its alien and to him unattractive attributes. Mr. Roosevelt, on the whole, thought that he could cajole Russia and even induce her to be assimilated into the great society which would embrace mankind; Mr. Churchill, on the whole, remained skeptical.

Mr. Roosevelt was imaginative, optimistic, episcopalian, selfconfident, cheerful, empirical, fearless, and steeped in the idea of social progress; he believed that with enough energy and spirit anything could be achieved by man; he shrank as much as any English schoolboy from probing underneath the surface, and saw vast affinities between the peoples in the world, out of which a new, freer, and richer order could somehow be built. Mr. Churchill was imaginative and steeped in history, more serious, more intent, more concentrated, more preoccupied, and felt very deeply the eternal differences which could make such a structure difficult of attainment. He believed in institutions and the permanent characters of races and classes and types of individuals. His government was organised on clear principles; his personal private office was run in a sharply disciplined manner. His habits, though unusual, were regular. He believed in a natural, a social, almost a metaphysical order—a sacred hierarchy which it was neither possible nor desirable to upset.

Mr. Roosevelt believed in flexibility, improvisation, the fruitfulness of using persons and resources in an infinite variety of new and unexpected ways; his bureaucracy was somewhat chaotic, perhaps deliberately so. His own office was not tidily organised, he practised a highly personal form of government. He maddened the advocates of institutional authority, but it is doubtful whether he could have achieved his ends in any other way.

These dissimilarities of outlook went deep, but both were large enough in scope and both were genuine visions, not narrowed and distorted by personal idiosyncrasies and those disparities of moral standard which so fatally divided Wilson, Lloyd George, and Clemenceau. The President and the Prime Minister often disagreed; their ideals and their methods were widely different; in some of the memoirs and gossip of Mr. Roosevelt's entourage much has been made of this; but the discussion, at all times, was conducted on a level of which both heads of government were conscious. They may have opposed but they never wished to wound each other; they may have issued contrary instructions but they never bickered; when they compromised, as they so often did, they did so without a sense of bitterness or defeat, but in response to the demands of history or one another's traditions and personality.

Each appeared to the other in a romantic light high above the battles of allies or subordinates: their meetings and correspondence were occasions to which both consciously rose: they were royal cousins and felt pride in this relationship, tempered by a sharp and sometimes amused, but never ironical, perception of the other's peculiar qualities. The relationship born during the great historical upheaval, somewhat aggrandised by its solemnity, never flagged or degenerated, but retained a combination of formal dignity and exuberant high spirits which can scarcely ever before have bound the heads of states. Each was personally fascinated not so much by the other, as by the idea of the other, and infected him by his own peculiar brand of high spirits.

The relationship was made genuine by something more than even the solid community of interest or personal and official respect or admiration—namely, by the peculiar degree to which they liked each other's delight in the oddities and humours of life and their own active part in it. This was a unique personal bond, which Harry Hopkins understood and encouraged to the fullest degree. Mr. Roosevelt's sense of fun was perhaps the lighter, Mr. Churchill's a trifle grimmer. But it was something which they shared with each other and with few, if any, statesmen outside the Anglo-American orbit; their staffs sometimes ignored or misunderstood it, and it gave a most singular quality to their association.

Mr. Roosevelt's public utterances differ by a whole world from the dramatic masterpieces of Mr. Churchill, but they are not incompatible with them in spirit or in substance. Mr. Roosevelt has not left us his own account of his world as he saw it; and perhaps he lived too much from day to day to be temperamentally attracted to the performance of such a task. But both were thoroughly aware of their commanding position in the history of the modern world, and Mr. Churchill's account of his stewardship is written in full consciousness of this responsibility.

It is a great occasion, and he treats it with corresponding solemnity. Like a great actor—perhaps the last of his kind—upon the stage of history, he speaks his memorable lines with a large, unhurried, and stately utterance in a blaze of light, as is appropriate to a man who knows that his work and his person will remain the object of scrutiny and judgment to many generations. His narrative is a great public performance and has the attribute of formal magnificence. The words, the splendid phrases, the sustained quality of feeling, are a unique medium which convey his vision of himself and of his world, and will inevitably, like all that he has said and done, reinforce the famous public image, which is no longer distinguishable from the inner essence and the true nature of the author: of a man larger than life, composed of bigger and simpler elements than ordinary men, a gigantic historical figure during his own lifetime, superhumanly bold, strong, and imaginative, one of the two greatest men of action his nation has produced, an orator of prodigious powers, the saviour of his country, a mythical hero who belongs to legend as much as to reality, the largest human being of our time.

Leopold Amery: Churchill and Lloyd George[4]

Churchill's friend and colleague Leopold Amery compared Churchill and Lloyd George in an essay which was first published in 1954.

No one, in a democratic country like ours, can be a great war leader who has not the gift of inspired and inspiring utterance. Lloyd George was a natural orator whose speeches owed far less to preparation than to the response of the audience before him. They served his purpose admirably in dealing with difficult industrial audiences, as well as with great popular demonstrations or with a crowded House of Commons. But they were essentially for the occasion. Churchill's oratory is of a very different type. It is the result of the transformation, by long years of effort and practice, of a purely literary rhetoric into an eloquence as easy as it is lofty; an eloquence as effective over the wireless or in cold print as to his immediate audience. It served him, not only to voice the stubborn courage of the nation, but to inspire it with a deeper sense of its own history and to give it a nobler quality. Nor was it limited to his own people here and beyond the seas. Through all the long years of German Occupation countless secret listeners, from Norway to Greece, were encouraged in their resistance, or at least sustained in their faith, by the unshakable confidence in that strong mellow voice. . . .

Demosthenes once described the supreme quality and purpose of oratory as action. Both Lloyd George and Churchill were, above all,

[4] From Sir James Marchant, ed., *Winston Spencer Churchill: Servant of Crown and Commonwealth* (London, 1954), pp. 68-72. Reprinted by permission of the Rt. Hon. Julian Amery, who informed the editor that the origin of this essay was a wartime after-dinner discussion of Plutarch's technique of comparing characters. Leopold Amery, who knew both Churchill and Lloyd George extremely well, was Secretary of State for India and for Burma in Churchill's wartime administration. Vol. III of his memoirs, *My Political Life* (London, 1955), has many references to Churchill between the wars.

restless men of action for whom eloquence was only an instrument, and not an end in itself. Both were men of undaunted courage: Lloyd George the more swiftly resilient; Churchill more grimly and imperturbably resolute. Both like Odysseus, masters of device; the one snatching ideas from the atmosphere of the moment; the other drawing upon a long accumulated store of thought on the problems of war. In most other respects their characters and temperaments were in striking contrast.

Lloyd George's mind, like his career, was discontinuous in regard both to time and to ideas. He had, indeed, his local patriotism for Wales and the Welsh language. But no broader background of history and tradition, even as regards the principles of that Liberal Party into which he was born. His mind was, indeed, too quick and too open both to new ideas and to those of his political opponents to allow of any rigid consistency with any set of principles or with his own past. It was a mind of disconcerting agility. Lord Milner once said to me after a Cabinet meeting that the only thing like it was the knight of the chessboard—it moved in two different directions simultaneously, both unexpected. So quick was he in taking up the ideas of others that a favourite jest in the First World War was that the country was governed by two men, Lloyd George and the last person he had spoken to—a valuable quality in breaking through hierarchical obscurantism in the Departments, but not always conducive to good results or good feeling. In his eagerness to get things done, in his absorption in the ideas and methods of the immediate occasion, and in his complete forgetfulness of what he had thought or said before, he created an impression of clever unscrupulousness and intrigue which did not do him justice. He was the consummate natural actor who lived wholeheartedly in the part of the moment, with little thought for other parts he may have played before.

In all this Churchill is the very opposite. Born into a great family with a famous history and at the heart of England's ruling class, he imbibed from Gibbon and Macaulay that profound and vivid sense both of the fateful movement and of the romantic pageant of the history of nations and of Empires which has dominated his outlook. To play his part in that great drama was his natural and mastering ambition. Not any part that came along, but the particular part of leadership in some secular crisis; to reincarnate his great ancestor, or Chatham, or the younger Pitt; to stand out in history as the champion of English freedom against another Philip of Spain, or Louis XIV, or Napoleon. Meanwhile to make his mark in the politics of the day, as early as possible, with the great end in view. That dramatic sense of historic continuity has not been accompanied by Lloyd George's instinct for, and even anticipation of, the movement of contemporary thought. The supreme moments of history are outside the fluctuations of political opinion, and at such a moment he could truly interpret the heart and mind of his countrymen and of the Empire as no one else could have done. At other times he has often seemed to belong to another and earlier generation.

With this difference in intellectual outlook has gone a corresponding difference in their relations to those with whom they have had to work. Churchill has always been too full of his own original thought-world, too self-contained, to be much affected by the thoughts of others or to be even conscious of them, except, on occasion, as resistances to be overborne by force of argument and eloquence. Lloyd George had an almost uncanny faculty of sensing what others thought and felt, even before they knew it themselves, and of entering into their thoughts and feelings in order to assimilate them or else divert them by persuasion into the desired channel. There never was any man who lived so entirely by immediate reaction to his surroundings. I sometimes felt that if he had been placed in a completely empty whitewashed room he would, like a character in one of Henry James's stories, have disintegrated and dissolved into nothing. Churchill, in such a situation, might imperturbably continue rehearsing the next speech or the next chapter, or, if aware of the bare walls, seize upon the opportunity for the expression of his talent as a painter.

Each served the needs of his occasion. Only Lloyd George's driving impulse and power of all-round improvisation could have coped with the general unreadiness and confusion of the First World War. Only Churchill's trained knowledge and wealth of historic inspiration have matched the height of his achievement in the Second. Lloyd George rose to greatness kindled by the stress of circumstances as he found himself confronted by them. For Churchill the great event came, and found him prepared to shape it for his country's saving, prepared as no British Prime Minister before him; ready "to serve, full harnessed as of old, the days that are the destinies."

Sir Arthur Bryant: Churchill and His Chief of Staff[5]

*Sir Arthur Bryant has described the relations be-
tween Churchill and General Brooke (later Lord Alanbrooke),
Chief of the Imperial General Staff.*

That evening marked the beginning of the long partnership
between these two men. Brooke already realised how formidable its
difficulties must prove. As Commander-in-Chief, he had learnt something of his leader's lightning changes of mood, untiring, stubborn
will, and passionate intensity. "Difficult times with the P.M. I see
clearly ahead of me," he wrote in his diary on New Year's Day, "I
pray God to help me by giving me guidance as to how to handle the
situations which are certain to confront me." Even in his first week
of office, before Japan entered the war and Churchill sailed for
America, he had had a foretaste of his impetuous, stormy temper. It
had happened at a midnight Chiefs of Staff meeting, with the Lord
Privy Seal, Mr. Attlee, and the Foreign Secretary, Anthony Eden, in
attendance, when the Chief of Air Staff had tried to stop the Prime
Minister from committing himself irrevocably to a promise to trans-
fer ten squadrons from North Africa to Russia at the end of the
Libyan offensive. "This produced," Brooke wrote,

> . . . the most awful outburst of temper. We were told that we did
> nothing but obstruct his intentions, we had no ideas of our own and,
> whenever he produced ideas, we produced nothing but objections,
> etc., etc. Attlee pacified him once, but he broke out again; then
> Anthony Eden soothed him temporarily, but all to no avail. Finally
> he looked at his papers for some five minutes, then slammed them

[5] From Sir Arthur Bryant, *The Turn of the Tide, 1919-1943* (London,
1957), pp. 298-303. Reprinted by permission of Collins Sons & Co. Ltd. and
Doubleday and Company, and with the approval of Sir Arthur Bryant. His
sequel, *Triumph in the West* (London, 1959), should also be consulted.

together, closed the meeting and walked out of the room. It was pathetic and entirely unnecessary. We were only trying to save him from making definite promises which he might find hard to keep later on. It is all the result of over-working himself and keeping too late hours. Such a pity! God knows where we should be without him, but God knows where we shall go with him!

Yet when the Chiefs of Staff met next morning they were greeted with a memorandum from their unpredictable chief couched in almost identical terms to those they had begged him to accept the night before. He would browbeat his advisers, but, provided they stood up to him, he was not prepared to overrule them. It was his instinct to pursue the daring course, and, in his dealings with his Allies, the magnanimous one. And he was deeply suspicious of what he called "resistances," particularly from his Service chiefs. "Those damned planners of yours," he once said to Brooke of the Joint Planning Staff, "plan nothing but difficulties." He was always afraid that opportunities to attack would be lost, by excessive prudence, inertia, "the usual helpless negation." It was a legacy partly from his experiences as a young soldier and Cabinet Minister after the long Victorian peace, when many senior military commanders had been hidebound and obstructionist and when his imagination and adventurous spirit had been thwarted by conservatism and playing for safety. It was the legacy, too, of the bitter years when he had been a voice crying in the wilderness, vainly warning his countrymen against "the dangers of yielding to soft, easy and popular expedients and the dark places into which we have been led thereby." And it was an inherent part—however troublesome to his advisers—of his service to England. It had been Churchill's passionate and reiterated refusal to take "No" for an answer when "No" would have involved certain defeat that had placed his country for ever in his debt.

It was his duty as Defence Minister to probe and sift the official advice tendered to him by his Service chiefs—most of whom had been young lieutenants when he had first become a Service Minister thirty years before—and he would have been a different, and lesser, man had he spared them. In doing so he was instinctively testing their plans by making them oppose him and argue them out in the teeth of his powers of debate and invective. If he found himself convinced they were right, he would himself become the spokesman of the very arguments he had so fiercely criticised. Both consciously and unconsciously, he was always testing his subordinates by the sternest of tests. "How often," wrote Brooke, "have I seen Winston eyeing me carefully, trying to read my innermost thoughts, searching for any doubts that might rest under the surface." In the last resort, his decision and his alone stood between the nation and disaster. Even when he seemed most unreasonable and exacting, it was impossible, Brooke wrote, "not to be filled with sympathy for him when one realised the colossal burden he was bearing and the weight of responsibility he shouldered."

For the traits that made Churchill so hard to work for arose, not from lack of heart or consideration, but from absorption in his task of saving the nation and the single-mindedness with which he pursued his object. He had so much on his shoulders—so much more than any other man—that he had little time to consider the convenience of others. His mind, interested in everything pertaining to the human lot, cast a searchlight into every cranny of the nation's life: Nothing came amiss to it, and no one could predict—least of all the Ministers, bureaucrats and Service chiefs upon whose activities it was turned—when and where it would light. Two days after Pearl Harbor and on the day that the *Prince of Wales* and *Repulse* were lost, and when the entire British and American position in the Pacific was crumbling, this amazing Prime Minister dictated, *inter alia,* three searching minutes to ensure that sweet-rationing should not be introduced unnecessarily, that timber-felling companies should not be allowed to denude woodlands without consideration for the appearance of the countryside, and that young women in the A.T.S., serving with A.A. batteries, should not be roughly treated and should receive every kind of minor compliment and ornament for good service.

When it came to the planning of military operations this tireless energy presented those responsible with a most difficult problem. It was a part of Churchill's greatness—and of the human attributes that are the accompaniment and, at times, reverse of greatness—that he was constitutionally incapable of not intervening with his entire heart, soul and mind in any operation, great or small, of which he had cognizance, whether strategical, administrative or technical. And since, as Minister of Defence he was responsible to Parliament for the entire conduct of the War, and since there was almost no martial activity in which—himself once a soldier, a military historian, and at one time political head of each of the three Services—he was not intensely interested, it followed that his and the nation's official advisers were subject to his questioning, entreaty, interference and, when necessary, reproach at every hour of the day and night. Enjoying, despite his sixty-seven years, a wonderful and unflagging vitality and health, and possessed of boundless curiosity and of a boyish and, at times, almost impish pugnacity and zest, he subjected them, often without realising it, to a continuous, harrowing and exhausting, if stimulating, martyrdom. The extraordinary hours he persisted in keeping, in glorious defiance of conventional Whitehall routine, made their ordeal all the more severe, since, while they were forced on the one hand to carry out their administrative work as heads of their Departments during the ordinary hours of Service and bureaucratic practice, they were expected to share in the long and exuberant night-life of their chief who, spending most of the daylight hours of morning in bed, reading and dictating despatches and memoranda and giving audiences, and refreshing himself after his Cabinet and parliamentary duties with an evening siesta, awoke to full and volcano-like activity—ten times greater than that of any ordinary being—at the hour when most men, exhausted by the day's labour, were seeking recreation or sleep. In those hours of the night, often continued till three or four in the morning, there poured from him a never-ending stream of ideas, projects, questionings, information, anecdotes and commentary on life and human nature. More often he spoke of the war and of the many and resourceful ways by which he hoped to win it.

Yet on a man bearing an immense executive load, who had been working since nine in the morning at high pressure at office-desk and in committee, these midnight sessions imposed an immense strain. "As I look back on them," wrote Brooke of his visits to Chequers, "I remember best long drawn-out evenings and a desperate longing for bed as these evenings extended well into the morning hours. There were times . . . of intense interest, and one could be certain of boundless hospitality, but at the end of a very hard week's work to be kept up till the small hours of the morning was, to put it mildly, a very trying procedure." When the American Chief of Staff, General Marshall, stayed with the Prime Minister for the first time, and dinner was followed by a review of the war which

went on till 2 a.m. and then by a film which lasted till 2.45 a.m.,
"his face," Brooke wrote, "was a study. . . . He was evidently not
used to being kept out of his bed till the small hours of the morning
and not enjoying it much. . . . I wonder how he would have liked
to work permanently with Winston, and be kept out of bed three or
four nights a week." [6]

"My day starts at 9 a.m. and seldom finishes before midnight,"
Brooke told a friend, "whilst it frequently goes on till one or two in
the morning. . . . Have now finished two months as C.I.G.S. and it
feels as if it had been ten years!"

[6] *Diary*, 10th April, 1942. "He certainly had a much easier life of it with
Roosevelt; he informed me that he frequently did not see him for a month or
six weeks. I was fortunate if I did not see Winston for six hours." *Notes on My
Life*, V, 381. [Bryant's note.]

John F. Kennedy: "He Has Always Championed Liberty"[7]

Granting Churchill Honorary Citizenship of the United States, President John F. Kennedy said:

We gather today at a moment unique in the history of the United States.

This is the first time that the United States Congress has solemnly resolved that the President of the United States shall proclaim an honorary citizenship for the citizen of another country and in joining me to perform this happy duty the Congress gives Sir Winston Churchill a distinction shared only with the Marquis de Lafayette.

In proclaiming him an honorary citizen, I only propose a formal recognition of the place he has long since won in the history of freedom and in the affections of my—and now his—fellow countrymen.

Whenever and wherever tyranny threatened, he has always championed liberty. Facing firmly toward the future, he has never forgotten the past. Serving six monarchs of his native Great Britain, he has served all men's freedom and dignity.

In the dark days and darker nights when England stood alone—and most men save Englishmen despaired of England's life—he mobilized the English language and sent it into battle. The incandescent quality of his words illuminated the courage of his countrymen.

Indifferent himself to danger, he wept over the sorrows of others.

[7] From a speech broadcast on April 9, 1963 and widely reported in many British and American newspapers. Kennedy in his analysis of British Foreign Policy before 1939, *Why England Slept* (New York, 1940; reprinted 1961), pp. 65-66, refers sympathetically to Churchill's isolation before the outbreak of war, and how he was considered dangerous and "a little uncomfortable to have around."

A child of the House of Commons, he became its father. Accustomed to the hardships of battle, he had no distaste for pleasure.

Now his stately ship of life, having weathered the severest storms of a troubled century, is anchored in tranquil waters, proof that courage and faith and zest for freedom are truly indestructible. The record of his triumphant passage will inspire free hearts all over the globe.

By adding his name to our rolls, we mean to honor him—but his acceptance honors us far more. For no statement or proclamation can enrich his name now—the name Sir Winston Churchill is already legend.

Harold Wilson: "The Qualities Born in Him"[8]

In his broadcast to the British people immediately after Churchill's death, the Labour Prime Minister, Harold Wilson, summarized what he considered to be Churchill's three dominant qualities.

. . . In the first war, he one minute carried the awesome responsibilities of First Lord of the Admiralty; in another he found himself a controversial, defeated ex-Minister, who sought a new duty in Flanders. Between the wars, he held the strings of Treasury power as Chancellor—a few years later he was an outcast, when he warned of the dangers that Britain faced as the shadow of the jackboot menaced European civilization. And, in September 1939, when his forebodings were realized, every man serving in every ship, in the far-flung Royal Navy, already deployed in its war posture, was electrified by the three-word signal from the Board of Admiralty: 'Winston is back.'

But it was his leadership of that war-time team, that great united team—Ministers of all parties, commanders and fighting men, the men and women of ammunition factories and those who kept going the essential home services—each of them willing to submerge his own identity and interest in a great cause under his lead, it was that leadership and that response which saved Britain and saved freedom.

[8] From a speech broadcast in January 1965, reproduced from the British Broadcasting Corporation publication, *Winston Churchill: A Selection of Broadcasts* (BBC London, 1955), pp. 65-66. Reprinted by permission of the Rt. Hon. Harold Wilson. The Prime Minister's speech in the House of Commons on January 25, 1965, should also be consulted. In it he described Churchill as "one of the architects of the revolution in the humane administration of the country" and finely described his parliamentary oratory as "the conquering weapon of words fashioned for their purpose: to wound, never to kill; to influence, never to destroy."

164

In his war memoirs he tells of his 'profound sense of relief' when in the midst of the disasters of the battle of France he became Prime Minister. 'I felt,' he said, 'as if I were walking with destiny, and that all my past life had been but a preparation for this hour and for this trial. . . . Therefore, although impatient for the morning, I slept soundly and had no need for cheering dreams.'

The morning, and all the mornings, provided the proof. Those five years brought forth the qualities born in him, the qualities he had nurtured. First, the quality of indomitable courage. Never in the hour of greatest peril doubting ultimate victory, he could at once rebuke and inspire fainter hearts than his own. That inner certainty which enabled him to stand almost alone in seeing and warning of the danger, that certainty became an unshakable rock when it was Britain and the Commonwealth who stood alone.

Second, his power to evoke an undeniable response. Winston Churchill had through his power over words, but still more through his power over the hearts of men, that rare ability to call out from those who heard him the sense that they were a necessary part of something greater than themselves; the ability to make each one feel just that much greater than he had been; the ability which runs like a golden thread through our national history to inspire a slumbering nation so that it can call up those inner reserves of effort and of character which have never failed us when our very survival has been at stake.

Thirdly, the quality of humanity. The man who could move armies and navies and embrace the world in one strategic sweep could himself be moved to uncontrollable and unashamed tears at the sight of an old soul's cheerfulness in a shelter or of a street of devastated houses, at the thought of the human realities which lay behind the war communiqués.

It was his courage, his humanity, the response he evoked in our people that wrote in those war-time years that imperishable chapter in our history, a chapter which will always bear the title he gave to one part of that chapter, 'Our finest hour.' Far overriding and sustaining those qualities which marked his years of leadership was his great sense of history, of, in his own words, 'walking with destiny'—thinking there not so much perhaps of himself but of his country and of the Commonwealth.

His power over the written and spoken word, which has illuminated his own historical writings, was itself thrown into clearer relief by his sense of making history and writing history, not as distinct occupations but as part of a wider whole; and it is because of this that the words and deeds of Winston Churchill will form part of the rich heritage of our nation and of our time for as long as history comes to be written and to be read.

Now, his pen and his sword are equally at rest. The tempestuous vitality of a man who would have scorned the ease of a peaceful retreat has ended today in quiet, in peace, in stillness. But what every one of us can know is that Winston Churchill's life, his monumental achievements, have enriched forever not only our nation which he led, not only the world which he bestrode, but the hearts of each of us whose lives he touched with his greatness.

The New Statesman: "Incapable of Using Power Evilly"[9]

Our last assessment comes from the British left-wing weekly newspaper, The New Statesman.

Winston Churchill's formal education was a failure; he left school ignorant and unawakened. To his grief, his brilliant father largely ignored him and declined any course of instruction in politics. Thus, though born to a great historical tradition of public service, he was largely self-taught and self-formed, a process he accomplished as a lonely subaltern on the frontiers of empire. It is not surprising, therefore, that he never developed a coherent political philosophy, and in several respects his approach to politics was unsophisticated, even immature.

This led him into many errors and misjudgments. Though a good House of Commons man, he could not adapt himself to the party system. His lighthearted change of party and his brash approach to the problem of coercing Ulster laid the foundations for the deep distrust in which he was held, through most of his life, by orthodox Tories. He allowed himself to be out-manoeuvred over Gallipoli, the one stroke of strategic genius which, if sustained, could have shortened the war; instead, the incident confirmed his reputation for folly. Free trade made him join the Liberals. But he despised their anaemic Nonconformity and they, in turn, feared his belligerent view of life. At the same time, his unthinking imperialism, his eager acceptance of the class-war (as during the General Strike), his taste for direct action and his failure to comprehend the basic aspirations

[9] An anonymous editorial in *The New Statesman,* January 29, 1965, entitled "Churchill: The Great Outsider." Reprinted by permission of *The New Statesman.*

of British socialism made him anathema to the Labour Party for many years.

There were deeper shortcomings, which again could be traced to the lack of system in his upbringing. His early manhood he spent in India; but his heart lay in the Anglo-American world, and he showed a curious reluctance to improve, at close acquaintance, his knowledge of the empire about which he wrote and spoke so much. He dismissed Gandhi as a 'half-naked fakir,' and never accustomed himself to the inevitable process of imperial devolution. Most of the great mass-movements of his time left him unmoved and uncomprehending. He tried to stifle communism at birth and was puzzled by its resilience—until it presented itself to him in the person of Stalin, a conventional power-figure he could understand. It took the fall of Singapore to bring home to him the rising colour-consciousness of the East, and even then he saw the problem mainly in terms of military architecture.

But his unawareness of system and cyclical change gave him great strength as an empiricist. In moments of crisis he was unburdened by preconceptions or rigid beliefs. This made him the greatest man of action of his age. He saw 1914 not as the end of an epoch, but as a moment when the Fleet ought to be ready and at sea. Unlike the appeasers, he regarded Hitler not as a complex phenomenon to be placed in an elaborate historical context, but simply as a menace to civilisation—and he reacted accordingly. He was the first to scrap the ideological barriers when the Nazis invaded Russia, the first in the West to restore them—at Fulton in 1946—when Hitlerism had been destroyed. He offered union with France in 1940 as a straightforward alternative to imminent defeat; but turned his back on Europe in 1951, when the opportunity to create a rationalised structure presented itself. He was a great internationalist: but mainly in the interests of national self-survival. He was thus able to prolong Britain's existence as a leading power by an entire generation—perhaps two—and to preserve the freedom of countless millions to propagate political and social ideas he detested.

Many more sober statesmen saw his immense appetite for unregarding action as potentially dangerous. This was to misunderstand the man. Churchill was rash, but incapable of using power evilly. For a politician he had exceptional magnanimity, his flashes of anger yielding swiftly to the lure of comradeship. He loved battle but detested persecution. Underlying these characteristics was the one salient principle of his life: his passionate regard for British parliamentary democracy.

This may seem paradoxical in a man who was an aristocrat by birth and an outsider by temperament, and whose favourite companions-in-arms were outsiders like himself—Lloyd George, F. E. Smith, Beaverbrook and Cherwell. Churchill, indeed, was not a skilful electioneer and frequently found himself rejected. But this never dimmed his conviction that the British people, as a whole, formed a mature and wise corporation, who could be trusted to exercise their constitutional rights responsibly. He saw it as his duty and function to use his matchless courage, oratory and powers of leadership to extract from our people the best they had to give. By a grandiose accident of history, he was privileged to discharge that role in full measure.

Afterword

What stand out as Churchill's basic assumptions and beliefs? We have seen how he regarded man as capable of immense self-improvement. He took an optimistic view of human capabilities. He believed that men could combine to improve their material condition and that the state had a positive and constructive role to play in this combination. He felt that governments had a duty to their citizens, not only to protect them against foreign interference, but also to help them against unfair social irregularity and hardship. He also insisted upon the primacy of individual effort. He believed that within the framework of a state-protected system, individual abilities must be allowed free play, and indeed must be encouraged. He opposed any rigid division of social opportunities along class lines, and admired those who had risen from poverty to riches, or from a humble background to political eminence. He admired also the altruism of patriotic endeavor, and the refusal of threatened peoples to submit to superior power wielded unjustly. Indeed, Churchill's major service to mankind was to hold up the torch of democracy against the storm of dictatorship, and to stand alone for the unconquered world while other democracies wavered or stood aside, watching tyranny triumph without seeking to halt it.

Churchill had many detractors and the hostile legends about him are innumerable. Many circulate without being challenged, and are believed without scrutiny. We have seen how he was falsely considered to be a man who eagerly welcomed war and relished the thought of civil violence. Yet Churchill was a man of great sensitivity and compassion. He considered universal peace and social comfort to be the ultimate aims of free men. He rejected all political systems which restricted human liberties, or withheld freedom of speech and freedom from arbitrary arrest.

Churchill was a man of powerful imagination and wide talents. He could be blunt and brusque in stating his opinions. But we have seen how he believed in stating those opinions both as clearly, and as persuasively as possible. In his view, every policy of which he approved was capable of being explained in rational terms. He refused to accept the need to impose policies on a reluctant or disbelieving nation. "Tell the truth," he urged Stanley Baldwin, the Conservative Prime Minister in 1935; "Tell the truth to the British people. They are a sturdy people and a robust people." This was the essence of Churchillian democracy. A nation deserved to be treated with respect by its leaders. The truth, however stark or unpleasant, however complex or apparently inconceivable, ought always to be at the forefront of a politician's repertoire. Churchill practised this precept throughout his long and busy life. He spoke the truth as he saw it. He prepared his speeches with incredible care, writing every word of them himself, revising them minutely, filling them with accurate detail and blunt phrases. He could often be wrong, but he was seldom hasty, flippant, or frivolous on the major issues of his day.

Churchill fought openly and publicly for the goals in which he believed: reduced military expenditure in 1900; a fair peace treaty for the defeated Boers in 1902; free trade in 1904; state aid to the underprivileged in 1906; the reduction of the powers of the House of Lords in 1910; a state-supervised nationwide insurance system in 1911 and an adequate defensive Navy in 1912 (never seen by Churchill as having any aggressive purpose whatsoever). He advocated a swift, efficiently fought war when war came in 1914, with minimum losses; a magnanimous peace in 1918; reconciliation with the Germans in 1919, and calling a halt to the advance of Bolshevism. He urged appeasement in Europe after 1925; a rallying of the democracies in the face of danger after 1933 and adequate rearmament to deter Nazi aggression before 1939. He had the courage to resist Nazi attack in 1940, and to stand alone against tyranny, while bearing no bitterness toward Russia or the United States for standing aside at that desperate moment for democracy. He argued in favor of magnanimity to the defeated foe in 1945 ("My hate ended with their surrender"); Anglo-American alertness against the expanding power of communism after 1945; the political unification of Europe in 1948; reconciliation with Russia after 1950 ("Jaw, jaw is better than war, war,"); and, after 1950, world appeasement based on the recognized strength of the democracies. These were some of his principal aims. Often they were unpopular. Often they were misunderstood. Yet he was always frank about them, and sought to explain them and defend them with all the powers of logical reasoning at his command. He never hid his opinions behind a smoke-screen of vague phrases or ambiguity.

Whatever our verdicts on any specific issue might be, one conclusion does seem incontrovertible: Churchill lived for politics. The main issues of public life stimulated and invigorated him. World affairs were in his bloodstream. For over fifty years his mind was focused on seeking solutions for the major problems of his time. It is for readers to judge whether the things he believed in and fought for were worthwhile; and, from the evidence at their disposal, to reach their own conclusions about Churchill's place in history.

Bibliographical Note

Are we dealing with the annals of a nation or with the biography of an individual?
—CHURCHILL ON KING ALFONSO XIII OF SPAIN

Churchill was a prolific writer, and wrote on a wide range of subjects. His books alone amount to over fifty titles, and he also wrote a large number of pamphlets and essays. From a careful reading of selected books by Churchill himself one can build up a clear picture of the full range of his ideas and achievements and of the history of his country and of two World Wars. His writings are lively, acute, detailed, and forthright. They are among the most powerful historical and political writings in the English language. Nor are they lacking in self-criticism or humor. For his attitude to war, and frank accounts of his own experiences and conclusions, three of his works are indispensable: *The River War* (London, 1900), *The World Crisis*, 5 volumes (London and New York, 1923-31), and *The Second World War*, 6 volumes (London and Boston, 1948-53). The last two have both been abridged, *The World Crisis* in one volume (London and New York, 1931) and *The Second World War* in one volume (London, 1959). For Churchill's speeches on social problems a useful collection is *Liberalism and the Social Problem* (London and New York, 1909). Some of his writings on world affairs were collected together by his son Randolph S. Churchill in *Step By Step* (London and New York, 1939); his speeches of 1936 to 1938, also edited by his son, were published in the United States as *While England Slept* (New York, 1938). His most important war speeches appeared in the United States as *Blood, Sweat and Tears* (New York, 1940); *The Unrelenting Struggle* (New York, 1942), and *The End of the Beginning* (New York, 1943). These speeches are among the finest examples of his literary genius. For those who wish to study his views on a wider range of topics, his memoirs *A Roving Commission* (New York, 1930), his essays *Amid These Storms* (New York, 1932), and his character sketches in *Great Contemporaries* (London, 1937), are vigorous and enjoyable. For a complete list of his books, pamphlets, articles, and introductions to other books see Frederick Woods, *A Bibliography of the Works of Sir Winston Churchill* (London, 1963), an important source for little known works by and about Churchill.

The fullest and most enjoyable anthology of his wit and wisdom is Kay Halle, *Irrepressible Churchill* (Cleveland, 1966). Churchill has to be seen as well as read, and to this end three comprehensive pictorial biographies can be recommended: Randolph S. Churchill, *Churchill—His Life in Photographs* (London, 1955); Richard Harrity and Ralph Martin, *Man of the Century: Churchill* (New York, 1962), and Alan Moorehead, *Churchill: A Pictorial Biography* (London, 1960). For a survey of cartoons Fred Urquhart, ed., *Winston Churchill: A Cartoon Biography* (London, 1955) should be consulted. There are two important collections of essays published in Churchill's lifetime, Charles Eade, ed., *Churchill By His Contemporaries* (London, 1953) and Sir James Marchant, ed., *Winston Spencer Churchill: Servant of Crown and Commonwealth* (London, 1954), both of which pass his career in review in many of its aspects.

Anyone seeking to recapture the mood of Churchill's wartime speeches should listen to gramophone recordings made at the time. A fine long-playing selection is available on: His Master's Voice; ALP 1435-36 and 1555-1563.

To see some of the variety of Churchill's moods one should look at film. A film which makes full use of newsreel material, and which (despite some poor reconstruction and inaccuracies) gives a vivid moving-picture of Churchill's career is *The Valiant Years,* produced by Jack Le Vien at Metro Goldwyn Mayer.

Although more than a hundred books about Churchill have been published since 1904, there is as yet no first-class full-length biography. A short and simple introduction is Martin Gilbert, *Winston Churchill* (New York, 1967). Longer and equally sympathetic accounts of his career are given in Virginia Cowles, *Winston Churchill —The Era and The Man* (London, 1953) and A. L. Rowse, *The Later Churchills* (London, 1958). The richest documentation for any great man's early life is given in the main and companion volumes of Randolph S. Churchill, *Winston S. Churchill: Youth 1874-1900* (Boston, 1966): subsequent volumes will take the story to Churchill's death in similar detail, and will become the standard documented source for Churchill's life. Two other books which deal comprehensively with the early period are Peter de Mendelssohn, *The Age of Churchill* (London, 1961), and Lady Violet Bonham-Carter, *Winston Churchill* (New York, 1965). Extremely critical biographies have been written by Emrys Hughes, *Winston Churchill: British Bulldog*

(New York, 1955), Francis Neilson, *The Churchill Legend* (New York, 1954), and David Thompson, *The Yankee Marlborough* (1959). These three provide representative examples of the criticism which Churchill often aroused.

Books which contain useful critical assessments of Churchill at important moments of his career are: Bentley Gilbert, *The Evolution of National Insurance in Great Britain* (London, 1966); Trumbull Higgins, *Winston Churchill and the Dardanelles* (London, 1963); Lord Beaverbrook, *Men and Power* (London, 1956) and *The Decline and Fall of Lloyd George* (London, 1963); Isaiah Berlin, *Mr. Churchill in 1940* (Boston, 1964); Trumbull Higgins, *Winston Churchill and the Second Front* (Oxford, 1957); Sir Arthur Bryant, *Turn of the Tide* (London, 1957) and *Triumph in the West* (London, 1959); Herbert Feis, *Churchill-Roosevelt-Stalin* (Oxford, 1957); and Lewis Broad, *The War That Churchill Waged* (London, 1960).

Among the many memoirs and biographies with interesting references to Churchill are Kenneth Young, *Arthur James Balfour* (London, 1963); H. H. Asquith (Lord Oxford and Asquith), *Memories and Reflections* (London, 1928); Roy Jenkins, *Asquith* (London, 1964); Lord Birkenhead, *Halifax* (London, 1965); Macleod and Kelly, *The Ironside Diaries* (London, 1962); Harold Nicolson, *Diaries and Letters, 1930-39* (London, 1966); Lord Ismay, *Memoirs* (London, 1960); Lord Montgomery, *Memoirs* (London, 1958); and Lord Chandos, *Memoirs* (London, 1962).

Serious historical perspectives are still lacking, even though some historians have, since Churchill's death, given vent to various biases. Goronwy Rees, "After the Ball Was Over" and Sir Basil Liddell Hart, "Churchill in War," both in *Encounter* (1966), sought to reduce Churchill's stature, but more by a combination of innuendo and overstatement than by careful historical analysis. Goronwy Rees was answered in *Encounter* by A. L. Rowse, "Churchill Considered Historically," and by Kenneth Young, "Off the Ball or Churchill Ill-considered" (1966). With Randolph S. Churchill's multi-volumed *Winston S. Churchill* probably completed by 1971, there will be no lack of primary material on which to base subsequent studies.

Index

Addison, Dr. Christopher, politician, 114

Agamemnon, 95

Amery, Leopold, Conservative politician, 142, 154-156

Antwerp, the defense of, 8-9, 90, 113, 118, 124

Appeasement, 46, 171

Aristotle, Greek philosopher, 113

Asquith, Baroness (Lady Violet Bonham-Carter), 142, 144-149

Asquith, Dame Margot, 146

Asquith, H. H., Liberal Prime Minister, 88-91, 103, 119, 144-146

Atlantic, battle of, 74

Attlee, Clement, Labour politician, at Dardanelles, 9; Lord Privy Seal, 157

Baldwin, Stanley, Conservative Prime Minister, 12, 42, 109, 121, 123, 126, 129-130, 135, 146, 171

Balfour, A. J., Conservative Prime Minister, 81, 85; elder statesman, 89, 94, 100

Barnes, George, Labour politician, 120

Beaverbrook, Lord, politician and newspaper proprietor, 105-106, 109, 133, 169

Berlin, Sir Isaiah, British philosopher, 142, 150-153

Bevan, Aneurin, Labour politician, 134

Birkenhead, First Earl of (F. E. Smith), Conservative politician, 29, 88, 111-116, 169

Blunt, Wilfrid Scawen, anti-imperialist, 41-42, 80

Bolshevism, 10-11, 70, 113

Boothby, Robert, Conservative politician, 124

Bracken, Brendan, Conservative politician, 124

Britain, Battle of, 61-62, 151

British General Strike of 1926, 11-12, 110, 121, 167

Brockway, Fenner, Labour politician, 106, 107-108

Brodrick, St. John, Secretary of State for War, 23, 79-80

Brooke, Alan (Lord Alanbrooke), British general, 157-161

Bryant, Sir, Arthur, British historian, 142, 157-161

Burke, Edmund, 68

Burns, John, Liberal politician, 31

Campbell-Bannerman, Sir Henry, Liberal Prime Minister, 102, 104

Carson, Sir Edward, Conservative politician, 100, 114

Cartland, Ronald, Conservative politician, 28

Cecil, Lord Robert, Conservative politician, 98

Chamberlain, Joseph, Unionist politician, 40, 80, 83, 102

Chamberlain, Neville, Conservative politician, 126; Prime Minister, 127, 132, 135

Chatham, Earl of, British Statesman, 94, 113, 155

Cherwell, Lord, British scientist, 169

"Churchill Must Go," 135-137

Churchill, John, Duke of Marlborough, victorious general, 1, 95, 110-111, 125, 155

Churchill, Lord Randolph, Conservative politician, 2, 76, 79, 80, 83-84, 85, 96, 112, 146

Churchill, Randolph S., historian and journalist, 142, 174, 175

Churchill, Winston Leonard Spencer, chronology of his life, 14-15; his abilities, 75-77, 82-83, 89-90, 96-97, 105-106, 113-115, 117-119, 122-123, 124-125, 132-133, 137-141, 164-165, 170-172; his ambitions, 76-79, 95-96, 104, 113, 119; his beliefs, 13, 170-172; his critics, 6-12, 77-78, 79-80, 81, 83-84, 88-89, 97-111, 120-124, 129-131, 134, 136-137, 145, 167-168; his friendships, 79, 87, 92-93, 102-

177

103, 112, 119, 148, 152-153, 168, 169;
his future, 85-86, 88-89, 98-99, 109-111,
116, 124-125, 136-37; opinions of, by
others, age twenty-three, 75-79, age
thirty-four, 84-87, age forty-two, 94-99,
age fifty, 112-116, age sixty, 126-129;
Prime Minister, 59-74
Clemenceau, Georges, French Prime Minister, 125
Clynes, J. R., Labour politician, 120
Conservative Party, Churchill attacks, 4;
Churchill moves towards, 105-106; complacent, 3; its hostility undiminished, 123-124, 126; retaliates against Churchill, 79-80, 81, 90-91, 99-103
Cortes, Conqueror of Mexico, 110

D'Abernon, Lord, British diplomat, 116-120
Dalton, Hugh, Labour politician, 8
Dardanelles, British attack on, 8-9, 90-91,
102-103, 109-110, 111, 113, 118, 124,
167
Demosthenes, Greek orator, on oratory,
154; on statesmen and politicians, 13
Disarmament, 23-24
Disraeli, Benjamin, Conservative Prime Minister, 3
"Down with Winston Churchill," 121
Drake, Sir Francis, buccaneer and patriot,
61
Dunkirk, evacuation of, 59-60, 73, 150

Eden, Anthony, Foreign Secretary, 157

Fairies, the good and the grim, 110, 129-130
Fischer, Louis, American writer, 131-132
Fishes, awaiting German invasion, 63, 149
France, 26, 29, 46-47, 51, 60-61, 63-65,
168
Franco, Spanish Caudillo, 129

Gallipoli (see Dardanelles)
Gambetta, French statesman, 65
Gardiner, A. G., journalist, 84-87, 93-99
Germains, Victor, journalist, 106, 108-111
Germany, Churchill's attitude towards, 12,
24-26, 46-48, 51, 54-55, 87-88, 128, 171
Gibb, Andrew Dewar, soldier, lawyer, and
Scottish nationalist, 91-93
Gibbon, British historian, 155
Goya, 119

Grey, Sir Edward, British Foreign Secretary,
74, 88, 89
Gwynne, Stephen, journalist, 114

Haig, Sir Douglas, British general, 114
Hankey, Sir Maurice, civil servant, 89-90
Henderson, Arthur, Labour politician, 120
Herbert, Sir Alan, Independent Member of
Parliament, 37n, 135-136
Hitler, Adolf, on Churchill, 130-131; Churchill's warnings about, 3, 129, 132, 168;
at war with Britain, 59-74
Hopkins, Harry, U.S. Emissary, 153
Hore-Belisha, Leslie, Liberal politician, 137-141
House of Lords, under attack, 35-36, 171

India, British Empire in, 11, 39, 41-45, 127,
129, 132, 168
Inskip, Sir Thomas, Conservative politician,
123
Insurance, Churchill a leading advocate of,
5, 33, 171
Irish settlement of 1922, Churchill's important part in securing, 124
Iron Curtain, the, 55-57

Jackson, Stonewall, general, 96
James, Henry, novelist, 84, 156
Japan, 73-74
Jerome, Jennie, Churchill's mother, 2
Jerome, Leonard, Churchill's grandfather,
1-2, 68
Jewish National Home, Churchill favors, 13
Johnson, Dr., conversationalist, 115

Kennedy, John F., U.S. President, 142, 162-163
Kitchener, Lord, Secretary of State for War,
9, 89, 90-91, 98

Labour Party, 3, 107-108, 109, 120-124,
137
Lafayette, Marquis de, honorary citizen of
the United States, 162
Law, Andrew Bonar, Conservative politician,
100, 104, 116
League of Nations, the, 52-53
Lenin, V. I., Bolshevik leader, 10
Liberal Party, passes out of existence, 126;
potentially vigorous, 3
Lincoln, Abraham, 98

Lloyd George, Dame Margaret, 140
Lloyd George, David, Liberal politician, 3-5, 88, 90-91, 96, 98; Prime Minister, 99-105, 109, 111, 114-115, 132, 142, 152, 154-156, 169
London, German bombing of, 62
Lothian, Lord, politician and diplomat, 150
Louis XIV, King of France, 1, 156
Loyalty, believed to be absolute, 148; Churchill's alleged lack of, 89; considered his dominant quality, 124-125

Macaulay, T. B., British historian and essayist, 78, 155
MacCallum Scott, A., Liberal politician, 81-83
MacDonald, Ramsay, Labour Prime Minister, 109, 121-122
Marlborough, Ninth Duke of, 79, 88
Marshall, American Chief of Staff, 160
Montgomery, Viscount, British general, 133
Morley, John, Liberal politician, 112
Mussolini, Benito, Italian dictator, 74, 128-129

Napoleon Bonaparte, French Emperor, 61, 64, 95, 97, 112, 156
Nazism, 12, 54, 60, 63, 66-67, 69, 71-73, 128
Nelson, Horatio, British admiral, 61, 110-111
New Statesman, British weekly newspaper, 142, 167-169
Nicolson, Harold, politician and writer, 124-125
Nile, Churchill's plan for irrigation on, 40

Odysseus, 155
Omdurman, Battle of, 17-20
Oran, British sink French fleet, 73

Pétain, Philippe, Marshal of France, 60
Pitt, William, British Prime Minister during Napoleonic Wars, 155
Plugstreet, Churchill serves in trenches, 91-93, 114, 164
Plutarch, Roman historian, 154

Rearmament, 54, 122-123
Riddell, Lord, newspaper proprietor, 87
Roosevelt, Franklin D., U.S. President, 57, 69, 142, 151-153, 161n

Roosevelt, Theodore, U.S. President, 83-84
Rosebery, Lord, Liberal Prime Minister, 41, 78
Rothermere, Lord, newspaper proprietor, 109
Rowse, A. L., British historian, 11
Ruskin, John, 97

Salisbury, Lord, Conservative Prime Minister, 80, 85
Salter, Sir Arthur, politician and administrator, 125
Science, and the future, 58; and peace, 49; and war, 52
Seely, J. B., Liberal politician, 89
Sheean, Vincent, American writer, 126-129
Shinwell, Emanuel, Labour politician, 120-124
Sinclair, Sir Archibald, Liberal politician and Churchill's adjutant in 1916, 92
Snowden, Philip, Labour politician, 121-122
Social reform, Churchill advocates, 4-6, 30-35
Soviet Union, Hitler's invasion of, 70-73, 74, 168
Spain, civil war, 129
Stalin, Joseph, 55
Steevens, G. W., journalist, 75

Taylor, A. J. P., English historian, 8-9
Times, The, British newspaper, attacks Churchill, 7, 87; supports Churchill, 6
Tonypandy, riots at, 7-8, 37-38

Unemployment, 5
United States, the, Churchill appeals to, 67-70; invaded by Japan, 73-74

Valentine, Alan, President of Rochester University, 67
Vanderbilt, Consuelo, American heiress, Duchess of Marlborough, 79

War, Churchill's view on, 2, 16-29; in the future, 51-52; "jaw-jaw" better than, 171; no cause for, 46-48; "very dangerous," 114
Warrant, for Churchill's arrest, 98-99
Wellington, Duke of, British general and Prime Minister, 110-111

Wells, H. G., British novelist and publicist, 106-107, 136-137

Whitman, Walt, American poet, 96-97

Wilson, Harold, Labour Prime Minister, 142, 164-166

Wilson, Woodrow, U.S. President, 152

"Winston's Folly," Churchill credited with, 124; tanks known as, 114-115

World, New York newspaper, defends Churchill, 87-88

World War I, Churchill and, 25-28, 88-105, 113-115, 118-119

DATE DUE